IN SPIRIT AND IN TRUTH

IN SPIRIT AND IN TRUTH

A Guide to Praying

Martha Graybeal Rowlett

The Upper Room
Nashville, Tennessee

In Spirit and In Truth

Scripture quotations not otherwise identified are from the Revised Standard Version of the Bible, copyrighted 1946, 1952, and © 1971 by the Division of Christian Education, National Council of the Churches of Christ in the United States of America, and are used by permission.

Scripture passages designated TEV are from the *Good News Bible, The Bible in Today's English Version*, copyright by the American Bible Society 1966, 1971, © 1976, and are used by permission.

Any scripture passage designated AP is the author's paraphrase.

The prayer of confession on page 18 and the prayer of thanksgiving on page 21 are adapted from *The Book of Worship for Church and Home*. Copyright © 1964, 1965 by The Board of Publication of The Methodist Church, Inc. Used by permission.

Selected lines from "The Order for the Administration of the Sacrament of The Lord's Supper or Holy Communion" are from *The Book of Hymns*. Copyright © 1964, 1966 by The Board of Publication of the Methodist Church, Inc. Used by permission.

Selected lines from "In Christ There Is No East or West" were written by John Oxenham (1852–1941). Used by permission of Desmond Dunkerley.

Selected lines from "O How Glorious, Full of Wonder" were written by Curtis Beach. Words copyright © 1958, 1981 The Pilgrim Press. Reprinted with permission from *Everflowing Streams: Songs for Worship*, ed. Ruth C. Duck and Michael G. Bausch.

The poem "Opening" by J. Barry Shepherd is reprinted from *Diary of Daily Prayer*, copyright 1975, Augsburg Publishing House. Used by permission.

Selected lines from "The Little Gate to God" by Walter Rauschenbusch are reprinted from *A Rauschenbusch Reader*, edited by Benson Y. Landis and H. E. Fosdick. Used by permission of Harper & Row, Publishers, Inc.

"The Twelve Steps" is reprinted from *Twelve Steps and Twelve Traditions*. Used by permission of A. A. World Services, Inc.

"Who Am I?" is reprinted with permission of Macmillan Publishing Co., Inc., from *Letters and Papers from Prison*, Revised, Enlarged Edition, by Dietrich Bonhoeffer. Copyright © 1953, 1967, 1971 by SCM Press Ltd.

Book and Cover Design: Jim Bateman
First Printing: December 1982 (7)
Library of Congress Catalog Card Number: 82-50944
ISBN: 0-8358-0448-8

Printed in the United States of America

Contents

FOR
Robert J. Arnott,
my husband and friend,
whose support made this book possible

SESSION ONE: *Introduction to Prayer and Praying*

Prayer is the Christian's vital breath,
The Christian's native air.
—James Montgomery

Prayer in the Contemporary Church

Once upon a time, a group of people came together on a Sunday morning in a church sanctuary. An organist and a choir performed beautiful music. A member of the congregation read from the Bible. Announcements were made. A story was told to the children. The minister preached a sermon. An offering was taken. There was more beautiful music. Then the people moved to the church social hall for coffee hour. There had been no word of prayer spoken or sung anywhere in the service—no praise or thanksgiving, no confession of wrongdoing, no request for God's forgiveness, no petitions for personal needs, no intercessions for the needs of the world, no dedication of the offering, no prayer of blessing at parting. Many words *about* God had been spoken but no words *to* God. No one noticed the omission. A few people had a nagging sense that something had not been quite right, but they could not identify just what. The stimulation of the coffee and conversation soon put it out of their minds. Could this be a true story?

Once upon a time, these same people went their separate ways. On Tuesday, one of them, George Davis, went into the hospital. He was scheduled to have surgery on Wednesday morning for a recurring malignancy in his intestinal tract. In the middle of the night, he woke up trembling with fear. In desperation he rolled over, clutched his pillow, and cried, "O God, help me!" Anxiety about future days

7

of suffering swept over him. The more he thought about the negative possibilities of his situation, the more anxious he became. So he called the nurse and asked for a strong sedative to quiet his nerves.

On Wednesday afternoon, Susan Carter had a quarrel with her husband. It was a recurring quarrel—one in which Susan was becoming increasingly frustrated. Harry had smoked cigarettes for as long she had known him. But in the last year, as job pressures had mounted, it seemed that he constantly had a cigarette in his hand. Not only was it a nuisance around the house and a strain on the budget, but Susan was worried about Harry's health. Today, however, when she raised the issue again, Harry blew up and stalked out of the house. Susan sank into a chair with tears of frustration welling up in her eyes. Out of the swirling rush of emotion, a prayer emerged: "God, I give up. You stop Harry from smoking!"

The Jones family was accustomed to saying grace before the evening meal. As they gathered around the table full of steaming food, Mr. Jones scowled at his chattering children until everybody quieted down. Then he bowed his head and rapidly muttered the words of the grace he used every evening. The younger children were not sure what he was saying, for the words all ran together.

No one else in the congregation prayed that week. Could this be a true story?

Prayer, both public and private, plays a less than central role in the lives of most Protestant Christians. Protestants typically go to church to hear the sermon and the music and to see their friends. Much of the private experience of prayer is the "foxhole prayer" of desperation, the use of prayer as a magic charm, or prayer as empty ritual.

Prayer in the Life of Jesus

It is instructive to compare the role of prayer in our lives with the far more central place of prayer in the life of Jesus. The Gospels report that he prayed in the midst of his ordinary life. He left his disciples to go out alone into the desert early in the morning or up into the mountains at the end of a busy day to pray. He went out into the mountains "and all night he continued in prayer to God" (Luke 6:12) before he chose his disciples. He prayed alone. Sometimes he took his disciples with him (Luke 9:28; Mark 14:32–33). He prayed for other people. The mothers brought their children to him "that he might lay his hands on them and pray" (Matt. 19:13). He told Peter that he had prayed for him, that his faith might not fail (Luke 22:32). He prayed for his enemies. From the cross he prayed for those who crucified him, "Father, forgive them; for they know not what they do" (Luke 23:34). And he prayed for himself. The Gospels record words from the Garden of Gethsemane and from the cross. "Abba, Father, all things are possible to thee; remove this cup from me; yet not what I will, but what thou wilt" (Mark 14:36). "Father, into thy hands I commit my spirit!" (Luke 23:46) His followers remembered and preserved teachings that revealed the value of prayer to Jesus. Among the few lessons Jesus taught in the form of a commandment were his instructions to "ask, seek, and knock" as reported in Luke.

> [Jesus] was praying in a certain place, and when he ceased, one of his disciples said to him, "Lord, teach us to pray, as John taught his disciples." And he said to them, "When you pray, say: "Father, hallowed be thy name. Thy kingdom come. Give us each day our daily bread; and forgive us our sins, for we ourselves forgive every one who is indebted to us; and lead us not into temptation."
> And he said to them, "Which of you who has a friend will go to him at midnight and say to him, 'Friend, lend me three loaves; for a friend of mine has arrived on a journey, and I have nothing to set before him'; and he will answer from within, 'Do not bother me; the door is now shut, and my children are with me in bed; I cannot get up and give you anything'? I tell you, though he will not get up and give him anything because he is his friend, yet because of his importunity he will rise and give him whatever he needs. And I tell you, Ask, and it will be given you; seek, and you will find; knock, and it will be opened to you. For every one who asks receives, and he who seeks finds, and to him who knocks it will be opened. What father among you, if his son asks for a fish, will instead of a fish give him a serpent; or if he asks for an egg, will give him a scorpion? If you then, who are evil, know how to give good gifts to your children, how much more will the heavenly Father give the Holy Spirit to those who ask him!"
> —Luke 11:1–13

Prayer in the Early Church

It is also instructive to look at the role of prayer in the early church. The story of the birth of the church begins with a group of men and women gathered in an upper room in prayer (Acts

1:12–14). After Pentecost, the new converts "devoted themselves to the apostles' teaching and fellowship, to the breaking of bread and the prayers" (Acts 2:42). The first deacons were appointed to care for the needs of the growing community so that the Twelve could devote themselves to prayer and to the ministry of the word (Acts 6:1–4).

Paul reports that he has been praying for the members of the churches to whom he writes (1 Thess. 1:2), and he repeatedly asks them to pray for him (1 Thess. 5:25, Rom. 15:30, 2 Cor. 1:11, Col. 4:3). Sometimes this request is open-ended, sometimes it is specific. In prison, Paul spent his time in prayer and "singing hymns to God" (Acts 16:25). In his teachings, he commends the life of prayer. To the church at Philippi, he says, "Have no anxiety about anything, but in everything by prayer and supplication with thanksgiving let your requests be made known to God" (Phil. 4:6). To the Thessalonians, he says, "Rejoice always, pray constantly" (1 Thess. 5:16-17).

"Prayer is the Christian's vital breath,/The Christian's native air," says the popular hymn by James Montgomery. Another by Arthur Coxe proclaims the faith:

> O where are kings and empires now
> Of old that went and came?
> But, Lord, thy Church is praying yet,
> A thousand years the same.

Format for This Study

This study assumes the continuing importance of prayer in the Christian life. The pilgrimage to Christian maturity is both an inward journey and an outward journey, a matter of the heart attuning to God and the hand stretching out to the world. In recent decades, Protestant churches have put major emphasis on the journey outward, the work of the Kingdom in combatting poverty, hunger, war, sexism, evil, and suffering. The result has been a one-sided development of the Christian life and an impoverishment of the Christian church. A life of service not balanced by a life of devotion produces burned-out social activists, sterile institutions devoid of the Spirit, and programs of good works without the inner resources to sustain them.

The purpose of this study is not to call Christians away from the world. It is to call Christians to prayer so that there can be wholeness to the pilgrimage of Christian life and direction and fuel for the journey. The format of this study includes resources for both praying and thinking about prayer.

Resources for Praying

Martin Luther once said, "None can believe how powerful prayer is, and what it is able to effect, but those who have learned it by experience." The primary way in which one grows in the life of prayer is by praying. It is possible to talk about prayer, to describe much about it. But our prayers can go where our thoughts about prayer cannot follow.

Therefore, an integral part of this study is the experiencing of a daily period of personal prayer for the duration of the study. A pattern is suggested here for your consideration and modification according to your personal needs and circumstances. Saint Teresa of Avila has been quoted as saying that the best way to pray is the way you pray best. Each of us needs to create an approach that seems natural and that fits where we are. The pattern described here reflects centuries of experience in Christian devotion, and yet it is only one of the many possible patterns. The general outline is as follows:

1. Preparation and centering
2. Praise and adoration
3. Confession
4. Meditative reading of scripture
5. Petitions
6. Intercessions
7. Thanksgiving
8. Dedication
9. Silence
10. Benediction

The specifics of these steps will be described in more detail in Session Four with the question, "How Can We Pray?" You can begin to experience the pattern now and be ready to reflect on it later.

Preparation for prayer is important. You will need a quiet place and at least thirty minutes of uninterrupted time. If you plan to use a Bible, a prayer journal, or other devotional resources, they should be close at hand.

Position for praying depends on the person and the circumstances. Kneeling with the head bowed and the eyes closed has been a tradition in Christian worship as a symbol of humility before God.

Popular for private worship is the sitting position, in a straight chair with feet flat on the floor, body bent at the knees and at the hips at ninety-degree angles. The head should be at an angle to look straight ahead if the eyes are opened. All of the muscles of the body can be deeply relaxed in this position, so it lends itself to stillness. Some people prefer the yoga position, others stand, while still others lie down to pray. Reducing sense stimulation by closing the eyes is helpful to many people. Others find that looking at a religious object like a cross or crucifix helps focus attention.

Centering is a process of pulling the attention into a focus, so that the mind can move to the heart. Simple awareness exercises may help. You can begin by being aware of your feelings. Identify your own present state of being. How are you at this moment? What is it like to be you right now? Are you happy, angry, depressed, excited, relaxed, anxious? What are you feeling? If you keep a journal, you may want to write down your feelings. If your mind is spinning, take a few minutes to quiet the flow of your thoughts. One technique is to imagine your mind as a whirling system of turning wheels. Visualize the wheels slowing down until they are barely moving. Be aware of your body. Are you tense, feeling pain, tired, tingling? If your body is tense, intentionally relax your muscles. Focus on one part of your body at a time, the face, the neck, the shoulders, deliberately letting go of all of the tenseness there, letting it flow away.

Notice your environment, the sounds you can hear, the odors and fragrances you can smell, other signals of which you are aware. This helps you to center in the present moment, the here and now.

Attention to breathing can help you to grow quiet. Taking a few, slow breaths can make deep relaxation possible. Observe the gentle breathing in of cool air through the nostrils and into the lungs and then the breathing out of warm air. Awareness of this natural rhythm in your body, like waves washing an ocean beach, prepares the mind for the inner communion of prayer.

Initially, this centering process may take a few minutes. With practice, centering can be done more quickly and easily. It is good for the body as well as the soul.

In the process of centering, you may become aware of strong feelings, concerns so powerful that it is hard to relax or become quiet. If so, you can begin immediately to share these with God. You may need to spend your prayer time in an honest unburdening of your soul in God's presence, asking for what you need for yourself or desire for others and listening to what God may be saying to you in response. On other days, you may want simply to be quiet in the presence of God.

Another way to approach a time of private prayer is to use a guide for prayer. The same guide can be used each day with personal additions or modifications made in response to the promptings of the Spirit. The traditional forms of prayer all have a place in the personal prayer life. Adoration, confession, thanksgiving, petition, intercession, and dedication do not all need to be included in prayer every day. But it is helpful to use each of them on a fairly regular basis to be sure that your prayers are not one-sided.

The guides for daily prayer provided in this study begin with scripture sentences that draw our awareness to the presence of God with us and the purpose of prayer. The prayers are not intended to be complete in themselves. They are starting places for your own prayers. The use of ellipses (. . . .) in some of the prayers is symbolic of the open-endedness of all of the prayers and an invitation to you to "fill in the blanks" with the prayers of your own heart. You may want to keep a journal in a separate notebook with a page for each day. It is, of course, not necessary to write anything. The space can be symbolic of your personal, unwritten, and perhaps even nonverbal prayers.

The prayers in these guides draw heavily on scriptural themes and themes from the traditional liturgies of the church. These themes are expressed in simple, contemporary English. A conscious effort has been made to limit masculine references in connection with God by rephrasing some of the material in the second person. Since prayer is direct communication with God, this seems natural and appropriate.

A passage of scripture will be suggested for meditative reading for each day of the week. Scripture reading is one of the listening parts of prayer. The passages listed are chosen as resources in the process of learning to pray and to think about prayer. Read them with the expectation that the Holy Spirit may speak to you. Read until something strikes you. Stop and reflect as you feel led. If you are using a prayer journal, record insights, applications, and nudges from your reflection.

Members of a group studying together may want to pledge to remember each other daily in prayer. Plan some time for sharing in the group about your experiences in these daily periods of personal prayer. You can support and encourage and learn from each other.

Silence is suggested at the end of each period of prayer, a time for resting in God's presence. This may be the most awkward and difficult part of the experience at first, but give it a try. You may find that you like it!

Resources for Thinking about Prayer

This study assumes not only the importance of praying but also the importance of thinking about prayer. One possible reason for the contemporary neglect of the devotional life may be that there has been so little clear thinking about prayer. Our minds have been so shaped by the scientific revolution of the past two hundred years that we are embarrassed and uncomfortable in the face of practices that defy critical scientific analysis. Prayer thus becomes a meaningless vestige of the past, existing in the shadowy realm of magic and superstition. We may still go through the motions of prayer, but we are not sure what we are doing. Occasionally the human spirit erupts in desperate or extreme circumstances. Even then we are not sure we could explain or justify the experience to ourselves or to anyone else in calmer circumstances. We are hard put to give an account of the faith that is in us. This uncertainty about how to think about prayer may be an inhibition to the life of prayer; therefore, this study provides resources for trying to make sense of our experience of prayer.

Prayer is natural. We are created with the capacity to pray. God gives us the gift of this special communication. We do not have to wait to have a perfectly constructed, carefully analyzed theology of prayer before we begin to pray. We can simply accept the gift and pray.

But God has also given us minds with which to analyze our experience. Thinking about prayer is one way to grow in the devotional life. If we have not separated prayer from magic, thinking about prayer can help us to do this. If our prayer life is limited to a few memorized prayers learned in childhood, thinking about prayer can open a new world of possibilities. If our prayer life has been frustrating and discouraging, thinking about prayer may help to uncover the problems. There will be unanswered questions, of course, but there can be answered ones, too!

This process of thinking about prayer will be pursued with the use of four questions:
1. How can we think about God?
2. How can we think about prayer?
3. How can we pray?
4. What difference does prayer make?

14

Resources for answering these questions will be drawn from scripture, the tradition of the Christian church, reason, and experience. The scriptures will be from the Revised Standard Version of the Bible. The tradition will come from the hymns of the church, the prayers of church liturgy, and the prayers of a few great Christians. The theology will come primarily from the work of John Cobb and David Griffin, who have, in turn based their work on the philosophy of Alfred North Whitehead. The experience of many people who have written and spoken on the subject of prayer will be interspersed as testimony.

Material for each session will include a discussion of the question for the session, questions for reflection and discussion, and a guide for a period of daily personal prayer for each day of the week or the intervals between sessions.

This material is designed in five segments that can be used in five sessions. However groups may want to devote more time to each question. Scripture passages for personal devotional reading can be used for two or more days each without exhausting all of their possibilities. What has been provided here for one week can be used for two or more weeks. Study groups should feel free to adapt these resources to their own pace.

It is desirable to share this pilgrimage of thinking about prayer. Individuals can use the resources separately, but there are decided advantages to sharing the experiences with a group—or at least one "soul friend."

One last word needs to be said about the relationship of this material to public prayer. Prayer is essentially the same thing whether it is individual or corporate. This material is written with the personal devotional life in mind. However, most of what is said is applicable to corporate prayer as well.

QUESTIONS FOR REFLECTION AND DISCUSSION

1. What role does prayer play in your life? In the life of your Christian community? What role would you like prayer to play?
2. What blocks you from growing in prayer? What other problems have you encountered when you pray?
3. What helps you grow in prayer?
4. What unanswered questions do you have about prayers?
5. Are you willing to commit yourself to a daily period of thirty minutes for meditation and prayer while using this study guide?
6. Do you as a group want to make a commitment to pray for each other daily while you are using this study together?

A GUIDE FOR DAILY PRAYER: ONE

Preparation and Centering

Worship God in spirit and truth, for this is what God wants.
    —John 4:23 (AP)
God is present in the world today, making new the whole creation. I will rejoice and be glad in this day!
    —Psalm 118:24 (AP)

Praise and Adoration

Let all the people praise you, O God!
Your constant love fills the universe,
and your faithfulness is without limit.
Your righteousness is like the towering mountains;
Your justice is like the depths of the sea.
People and animals and all things are cared for by you.
How precious is your love, O God!
Your people find protection under the shadow of your wings.
We live on the abundance of good things that you provide.
With you is the fountain of life, and because of your
light we see light.
I praise your name, O God.
    —Psalm 36:5–9 (AP)

Confession

If we say we have no sin, we deceive ourselves, and the truth is not in us.
    —1 John 1:8

17

O God, you have set forth the way of life in your beloved son. I confess with shame my slowness to learn of him, my reluctance to follow him. You have spoken and called, and I have not paid attention. Your beauty has shown forth, and I have been blind. You have stretched out your hands to me through other people, and I have passed by. I have taken great benefits with little thanks. I have been unworthy of your changeless love. Forgive me of these and all my sins.
—Adapted from the "Wesleyan Covenant Service" in *The Book of Worship*

But if we confess our sins, God who is faithful and just will forgive our sins and purify us from our wrongdoing.
—1 John 1:9 (AP)

Forgive me, purify me, and guide me into life eternal. Amen.

Meditative Reading of Scripture

Day One—Philippians 4:4–7
Day Two—Exodus 33:7–23
Day Three—Romans 8:9–11
Day Four—Psalm 139:1–18
Day Five—Isaiah 49:14–16
Day Six—Romans 8:38–39
Day Seven—Luke 15:8–10

Insights from the scriptures:

Petitions

I pray for daily bread, the necessities of life.

Hear my prayer, O God!

I pray for health in body, mind, and spirit.

Hear my prayer, O God!

I pray for protection from all that might hurt or destroy me.

Hear my prayer, O God!

I pray for an awareness of your presence—inspiring, challenging, and giving me strength.

Hear my prayer, O God!

I pray for guidance in the way that leads to true joy.

Hear my prayer, O God!

I pray for. . . .

Hear my prayer, O God!

Intercessions

The following intercessions are adapted from the *Book of Common Prayer.*

I pray for the church. May all who are part of your church in the world be united in your spirit, speak the truth in love, and show forth your glory in the world.

I pray for peace. Teach the people of all nations the ways of justice and peace. Guide them in the ways of mutual respect and give them commitment to serving the common good.

I pray for our physical environment. Enhance our reverence for our hospitable but fragile earth. Teach us to live in harmony with the rest of creation and to use its resources wisely.

I pray for those whose lives are closely linked with mine. May they receive the good gifts you have in store for them. I pray especially for. . . .

I pray for those who suffer. Give them healing, comfort, courage and hope. Bring them to the joy of salvation. I pray especially for. . . .

I pray for. . . .

Thanksgiving

O God, the fountain of all goodness, you have been gracious to me through all the years of my life. I thank you for your lovingkindness which has filled my days and brought me to this time and place. You have given me life and reason and set me in a world which is full of your glory. You have comforted me with family and friends, and ministered to me through the hands and minds of other people. You have set in my heart a hunger for you, and given me your peace. You have redeemed me and called me to a high calling in Christ Jesus. You have given me a place in the fellowship of your Spirit and the witness of your church. In darkness you have been my light, in adversity and temptation a rock of strength, in my joys the very spirit of joy, in my labors the all-sufficient reward. You have remembered me when I have forgotten you, followed me even when I fled from you, met me with forgiveness when I turned back to you. For all of your good gifts, I give you thanks, O God.

    —Adapted from the "Wesleyan Covenant Service" in *The Book of Worship*

Dedication

Lord, make me an instrument of your peace,
Where there is hatred, let me sow love;
Where there is injury, pardon;
Where there is doubt, faith;
Where there is despair, hope;
Where there is darkness, light;
Where there is sadness, joy.

O divine master,
grant that I may not so much
seek to be consoled as to console;
be understood as to understand;
be loved as to love;

21

for it is in giving that we receive;
it is in pardoning that we are pardoned;
and it is in dying that we are born to eternal life. Amen.
    —Saint Francis of Assisi

Silence

Benediction

Glory to God whose power, working in us, can do infinitely more than we can ask or imagine: Glory to God from generation to generation in the Church, and in Christ Jesus for ever and ever. Amen.
    —*Book of Common Prayer*

SESSION TWO: *How Can We Think about God?*

"The greatest problem with prayer today," says John Cobb, "is the image of that to which it is directed" (*Religious Experience and Process Theology*). When we have no clear conception of what God is like, where God is to be found, and how God relates to the world, we are likely to be hesitant and limited in prayer. So the starting place for a discussion of thinking about prayer can very reasonably be some reflection on how we can think about God.

Our Concepts of God Can Always Grow

One way we can approach the challenge of thinking about God is to compare the experience to that of thinking about another person. There are some important similarities between these two experiences, but this is a limited and potentially misleading analogy. There are important differences as well. We will start with the similarities and note the limits to the analogy later.

What you think about another person and what the other person is are never exactly the same. We are never able to perceive everything that another person is. No one can ever know us just as we are. We may think that we know or understand another person well. But people who have lived together for more than fifty years acknowledge that there is always an element of surprise in the relationship, always something more to be learned about the other. This mystery of the otherness that can never be plumbed is even more true in our relationship with God. The being of God is beyond our comprehension. We can think many things about God, but our thoughts can never encompass all of the being of God.

One of the classics of Christian spirituality describes God as hidden completely from our view by a "cloud of unknowing." The anonymous fourteenth-century writer says that God's being is so much beyond our comprehension that our human language can never express that being. Even our thoughts cannot come near to what God is.

In the book of Exodus there are two stories about attempts made by Moses to comprehend who God is. In the third chapter, he asks for God's name. In the Hebrew culture, this was a way to ask for the key to God's identity. The answer he receives is "I am who I am" (Exod. 3:14). In the thirty-third chapter, he asks to see God's glory. He is permitted only a partial vision, and he is told that no one can see God and live (Exod. 33:18–20). God remains beyond our comprehension. There is always mystery and more to be known.

Our concepts of another person can change and grow. The first time I encounter another person, I may be scarcely aware of her or him at all. Those of us who live in larger towns and cities are exposed to many people whose presence we virtually ignore. We have almost no concept of other drivers on the highway, strangers in a crowd at a ball game, and sometimes even our neighbors down the street. If we do notice these people, we perceive superficial data such as age, sex, and race. If we are willing to commit time and energy to the process, and if the other person is willing to be known, it is possible to vastly expand this initial perception. The middle-aged man who delivers our mail each day may be discovered to be an affectionate and indulgent father to two lively teenagers, a regular Thursday night bowler, a whiz at growing tomatoes, and much more.

Likewise, our concept of God can grow. The scriptures, in fact, record that our ancestors in faith grew in their understanding of God over a period of more than a thousand years. One of the most fascinating developments is the conceptualization of how God was present with them.

As the Hebrews went out of slavery in Egypt into the wilderness, they perceived God's presence in a pillar of cloud by day and a pillar of fire by night. After the debacle at Mount Sinai with the golden calf, God sent an angel to be their constant guide. But Moses established a Tent of Meeting where anyone of the people could meet with God in time of need. When Moses entered the tent, the pillar of cloud would come down and settle at the door of that tent (Exod. 33:7–9). Later the presence of God came to be associated with a box or ark which contained objects of religious value. In the story of King David, the people, finally settled in their new land, considered building a permanent house for the ark, for God's presence (2 Sam. 7:1–27). Here an interesting transition takes place in the thinking of the people. God did not want a house of wood. God would create a "house"—the House of David. God's presence would be in this dynasty, and the Messiah would come from the House of David, since God was present in a special way in David's descendants.

In the New Testament, God is present in Christ. "In Christ God was reconciling the world" (2 Cor. 5:19). "The Word became flesh and dwelt among us, full of grace and truth; we have beheld his glory" (John 1:14). Later God's presence came into the church in the Holy Spirit. In Paul's letters, the Spirit dwells in the Christian (Rom. 8:9; 1 Cor. 3:16; Eph. 5:18).

J. B. Phillips wrote a popular book entitled *Your God Is Too Small* calling upon people to let their concepts of God grow. The "God is Dead" movement heralded not the death of God but the death of some old ideas of God that needed to be discarded anyway. The fact that the bumper sticker "God is not dead—she is black" is shocking to many people is a clue that there is plenty of room for our concepts of God to grow.

Ways We Grow in Our Concept of God

Continuing the analogy, we grow in our concept of God in ways similar to the way we grow to know each other. For example, if I have just become acquainted with you, there are several ways that I could get to know you. I could get to know you by experiencing how you relate to me. If you listen carefully to what I say, hear the feelings behind my words, and let me know that you hear and care, I will come to think of you as a kind and sensitive person.

The Hebrew people came to think of God as the one who led them out of slavery. Repeatedly in the Old Testament, God is introduced as the one who led the people out of Egypt. Who God is was partially defined in terms of what God did, the way the people experienced God. We continue to sing about our experiences with God in hymns such as Joseph H. Gilmore's song: "He leadeth me: O blessed thought! O words with heavenly comfort fraught!" We also speak about our experiences with God in familiar liturgies like The Korean Creed.

> We believe in the one God, maker and ruler of all things . . . the source of all goodness and beauty, all truth and love.
> We believe in Jesus Christ, God manifest in the flesh, our teacher, example, and Redeemer, the Savior of the world.
> We believe in the Holy Spirit, God present with us for guidance, for comfort, and for strength.

If we have experienced God as a comforting presence in a time of pain or sorrow or loneliness, than we can think of God as one who is close to us and who cares about us. If we have had a mystical "oceanic experience" of the oneness of all creation, then we can think of God as the one in whom the whole of creation has unity. If we have experienced the life and teachings of Jesus as guiding our value formation, then we can think of God in Christ as the way and the truth.

A second way I can come to know you better is through what others tell me about their experiences with you. In our scriptures and traditions, we have the record of centuries, thousands of years of the experience of people with God. The sum of the testimony in our Judeo-Christian heritage is a resource of incredible richness, adequate for more than a lifetime of firsthand experience.

A third way in which I can come to a fuller, clearer concept of who you are is indirect. It may be that if I am really to see *you*, my perceptions of the nature of reality will have to change. James Clavell, in his novels *Tai Pan* and *Shogun*, depicts Europeans making their first contacts with the people of China and Japan. These early adventurers thought of the Asians as uncivilized barbarians. In fact, Asian habits of personal hygiene and systems of community organization were in some ways more civilized than those of the Europeans. A knowledge of the long history and rich culture of these newly discovered countries would have given the explorers a different perception of their new acquaintances. Today Western crowds flock to Chinese art exhibits and Japanese automobile showrooms, reflecting how increased acquaintance has modified the Western understanding of the reality of Asia and the Western perception of the character of specific individual Asians.

As our perceptions of the reality of our universe expand, our concept of God can grow as well. In a world of space travel, it is no longer appropriate to think of God as up there in the sky. New understandings of the nature of reality coming to us through scientific research are not a threat to the existence of God, but a challenge to grow in our ways of thinking about God.

The best way for me to get to know you is if you choose to reveal yourself to me. If you decide that you would like for me to know you, and you decide to tell me about yourself, to show me who you are, then I have my best chance for growing in my concept of you. Christians believe that this is what God has done in Jesus Christ. God has come to be with us in Christ as a way of responding to the age-old request expressed by Moses, "Let us see your glory" (Exod. 33:18, AP). Christ is sometimes referred to as our "window on divinity," for in Christ we are able to see into the nature of God. For Christians, Christ is the supreme revelation. If we want to grow in our ways of thinking about God, we can attend to what God has chosen to share with us in Christ.

Further, it is part of the testimony of Christians that this revelation continues through the presence with us of the spirit of the risen Christ or the Holy Spirit. God's self-revelation was not just a one-time event.

One final use of this limited analogy may be appropriate to our purposes here. I do not need to wait until I get to know you perfectly and completely before I establish a relationship with you. In fact, if I do not establish some kind of relationship with you, my chances of getting to know you in any significant way are pretty slim. It is possible for me to begin to communicate with you when we first meet. My relationship with you and my concept of you can grow together. If I wait until I know everything about you before I begin to relate to you, I may just never get around to it. It is possible for us to worship that in the nature of God which calls forth adoration from us before we have our concepts of God all worked out. It is possible for us to share our concerns and to listen for the word of God without having our images crystal clear. It is possible to have a significant relationship with God, even to love God, without knowing everything there is to know.

27

God as More Than Personal Spirit

Thinking about God is also different from thinking about another person. It is easy for us to think about God as a person because so much of biblical imagery is personal. God walks in the Garden of Eden, bargains with Abraham, gets angry at Mount Sinai, talks to the prophets. It is easy to understand how Michelangelo could paint God on the ceiling of the Sistine Chapel as an old man with a white beard. There is something in all of us that needs to think of God as personal. "Personal" easily becomes "person." If God is a person, then the next logical step is to create God in our own image with a physical body. The masculine image of God's body is the product of the patriarchal society in which our faith has taken root and grown. A deity is usually identified with that which is most highly valued in a society. In some cultures, the god is female; in some it is an animal or tree or mountain. Our patriarchal ancestors saw God as a humanlike male. The long white beard is probably the product of the ancient association of wisdom with age.

But God is spirit. "God is spirit, and those who worship him must worship in spirit and truth," John reports Jesus as saying to the Samaritan woman at the well (John 4:24). The writer of the first letter to Timothy speaks of God as "immortal, invisible" (1 Tim. 1:17). This text has been set to music in one of the great hymns of the church by Walter Chalmers Smith, "Immortal, invisible, God only wise,/In light inaccessible hid from our eyes."

Thinking of God as spirit is not so difficult if we refer once again to the analogy of human relationships. When I relate to you, I relate to more than your body. We communicate through our bodies, our voices and ears, our movements and eyes, our sense of touch. But the kindness and sensitivity that I have come to know are expressions of your spirit. There is, however, a difference between our finite human spirit and the eternal divine Spirit. God is not just a larger disembodied version of our human spirit. God is not confined to the possibilities of personality.

Another way of saying this same thing is to say that God is more than personal. This means that God is at least personal, for God is able to communicate with the personal dimension of creation and to be involved in personal relationships. God is not impersonal. God can be addressed as a "Thou," a personal being.

HOW CAN WE THINK ABOUT GOD?

Because we know only two kinds of personal beings, male and female, and our language only provides for conversation about "he's" and "she's," we get caught in the trap of referring to God as "he." But God's being transcends sexuality.

God is spirit, and God is more than personal. Getting our minds around what it means to be more than personal divine spirit may be the toughest part of the process of thinking about God.

What more is it possible for us to think? For our faith to be healthy and effective, our perceptions of God must fit with our general experience of reality. They must be consistent with what we know about how the universe functions. To be Christian, our concept of God must be also scriptural. Poised as we are near the end of the twentieth century of the Christian tradition and at the end of the second century of the scientific revolution, what can we say about the nature of God that is both reasonable and Christian?

It is both Christian and reasonable to think of God as present with us in every moment. Primitive images of God have usually located God "out there" somewhere. "Out there" is often also "up there" in heaven. Much of our religious language projects this sense of distance between ourselves and God. Certainly God may be thought of as beyond us—up there and out there. But God can also be thought of as with us and within us.

In *Abandonment to the Divine Providence*, Jean-Pierre De Caussade wrote about the sacrament of the present moment, for, he said, that is where God can be found. De Caussade also wrote, "Faith sees that Jesus Christ lives in everything and works through all history to the end of time, that every fraction of a second, every atom of matter, contains a fragment of his hidden life and his secret activity." Later he adds that "God's action penetrates every atom of your body, into the very marrow of your bones."

John Cobb speaks of the absolute nearness of God. In his book, *God and the World*, Cobb says that "God is everywhere...God is immediately related to every place...there is nowhere one can flee from him." Using more technical language in *A Christian Natural Theology*, Cobb points out that, "Every other entity can be somehow distanced, either as temporally past or spatially separate, but God's presence is absolutely present. He is numerically other, and qualitatively, incomprehensibly other. But this other is spatiotemporally not distant at all. . . . We are literally in God and God is literally in us." The Jerusalem Bible translates part of Romans 8:9 as "The Spirit of God has made his home in you."

Dame Julian of Norwich became aware of this absolute presence of God. She is quoted as saying, "Then our Lord opened my spiritual eyes and showed me the soul in the middle of my heart. . . . Nor will he quit the place he holds in our soul forever—as I see it. For in us is he completely at home, and has his eternal dwelling" (*True Prayer* by Kenneth Leech).

The implications of this way of thinking about God are important for the way we think about prayer, especially for those who have groped around for God outside of themselves somewhere. Offering spiritual advice to Madame Guyon, a Franciscan friar said, "Madame, you are seeking *without* that which you have *within*. Accustom yourself to seek God in your own heart, and you will find him" (*The Meaning of Prayer* by Harry Emerson Fosdick).

Samuel Longfellow wrote a hymn that expresses the church's faith in this absolute nearness of God.

> God of the earth, the sky, the sea,
> Maker of all above, below,
> Creation lives and moves in thee,
> Thy present life through all doth flow.
>
> Thy love is in the sunshine's glow,
> Thy life is in the quickening air;
> When lightnings flash and storm winds blow,
> There is thy power; thy law is there.
>
> We feel thy calm at evening's hour,
> Thy grandeur in the march of night;
> And when the morning breaks in power,
> We hear thy word, "Let there be light!"
>
> But higher far, and far more clear,
> Thee in [our] spirit we behold;
> Thine image and thyself are there,
> Th' indwelling God, proclaimed of old.

It follows naturally to think of the God who is present in every moment in our inner being as knowing every detail of our lives. The psalmist gives poetic expression to this experience of God:

> O Lord, thou has searched me and known me!
> Thou knowest when I sit down and when I rise up;

thou discernest my thoughts from afar.
Thou searchest out my path and my lying down,
and art acquainted with all my ways.
Even before a word is on my tongue,
lo, O Lord, thou knowest it altogether.
Thou dost beset me behind and before,
and layest thy hand upon me.
Such knowledge is too wonderful for me;
It is high, I cannot attain it.

Whither shall I go from thy Spirit?
Or whither shall I flee from thy presence?
If I ascend to heaven, thou art there!
If I made my bed in Sheol, thou art there!
If I take the wings of the morning
and dwell in the uttermost parts of the sea,
even there thy hand shall lead me,
and thy right hand shall hold me.
If I say, "Let only darkness cover me,
and the light about me be night,"
even the darkness is not dark to thee,
the night is bright as the day;
for darkness is as light with thee.

For thou didst form my inward parts,
thou didst knit me together in my mother's womb.
I praise thee, for thou are fearful and wonderful.
Wonderful are thy works!
Thou knowest me right well;
my frame was not hidden from thee,
when I was being made in secret,
intricately wrought in the depth of the earth.
Thy eyes beheld my unformed substance;
in thy book were written, every one of them,
the days that were formed for me,
when as yet there was none of them.
How precious to me are thy thoughts, O God!
How vast is the sum of them!
If I would count them, they are more than the sand.
When I awake, I am still with thee.
        —Psalm 139:1–18

In the story of the selection of David as King, the Lord says to Samuel, "The Lord sees not as man sees; man looks on the outward appearance, but the Lord looks on the heart" (1 Sam. 16:7).

31

One conception of God that makes prayer difficult is the "top-level executive" image. It is not surprising that in a world of giant bureaucracies and multinational corporations, this kind of imagery should be a problem. We see top executives making only major decisions, surrounded by busy staffs who handle the details and the less important decisions. We hear that to make it to the top you have to know how to delegate. It is easy for that kind of hierarchical thinking to be transposed into our thinking about God. Such a God, of course, could not be bothered with us—unless, perhaps, we were desperate. We should only pray to such a God about the major problems of the world—wars, droughts, hunger, injustice. Certainly there is no place for the ordinary cares and details of our lives.

Yet the early church remembered Jesus saying, "Your father knows what you need before you ask him" (Matt. 6:8). God knows us even better than we know ourselves. "Even the hairs of your head are all numbered" (Matt. 10:30).

The God whose creative power has made possible the whole universe is present with us, in us, in every split second of our existence, knowing us behind all of our self-doubts, masks, and pretensions, knowing us more honestly and intimately than we know ourselves.

Another way of saying the same thing is to say that truth can only be perceived from the perspective of God. You cannot know me completely. Even I do not really know myself. Only God knows the full reality of who I am. The same is true about the condition of the world at any one time. There is important religious insight in the old cliché, "Only God knows!"

This Spirit which is so near to us and knows us so well is beyond us and beyond all of creation. The word *transcendent* is an important word in the Christian tradition of thinking about God. It communicates that the God who dwells *in* the creation also exists *beyond* the creation. God is in the world, but the world does not contain all of God.

Oliver Wendell Holmes captures this vision of the combination of the greatness and the nearness of God in a hymn:

> Lord of all being, throned afar,
> Thy glory flames from sun and star;
> Center and soul of every sphere,
> Yet to each loving heart how near!

HOW CAN WE THINK ABOUT GOD?

Sometimes in worship Christians become so conscious of God's nearness that they develop a kind of cozy, "chummy" relationship with God that does not seem to take into account God's transcendence. This image of God almost resembles the ancient gods who were thought to belong to one particular tribe and to protect only their interests. God is not our private possession but is the God of all creation. In *Reality and Prayer,* John Magee points out:

> We are led by Jesus to dare to call God "Father" in an intimate colloquy of the soul. . . . Yet we entirely miss the meaning of this intimate communion unless it is set against the awesome vastness of the Adorable Majesty. . . . The intimate and the ultimate . . . are qualities that mutually enrich one another. Only in the wedding of these polar truths is the mystery of God's gracious presence saved from stupid sentimentality. This does not mean that we are to be less intimate, but rather that we are to know this intimacy against the background of ultimacy.

It is both Christian and reasonable to say that it is in God that we experience our unity with the whole of creation. God is present in every moment to every part of the whole universe. In that copresence we have our oneness with each other. The universal nature of God is clearly expressed in John Oxenham's hymn:

> In Christ there is no east or west,
> In him no south or north;
> But one great fellowship of love
> Throughout the whole wide earth.
>
> In [God] shall true hearts everywhere
> Their high communion find;
> [God's]service is the golden cord
> Close binding [humankind].

Marshall McLuhan coined the phrase "the global village," giving us a new way to refer to our increasingly close-knit world community. Space explorations have given us photographs of the earth and a new perception of our common destiny as a human race. But our common life is not a simple matter of physical proximity and interdependence. We are one with each other because of our common relationship to God. Paul Tillich describes God as "the ground of being." In *Science and the*

Modern World, Alfred North Whitehead speaks of our existence in the universe as a matter of "through and through togetherness..." He says that God is "the binding element in the world" (*Religion in the Making* by Alfred North Whitehead). In God everything is interrelated with everything else.

God as Creative-Responsive Love

Now we come to the most incredible part of all. The Christian revelation of God in Christ has been summed up in three words, "God Is Love" (1 John 4:8). The Psalms, the hymnbook of the Old Testament, sing God's praises for "steadfast love" which is abundant (Psalm 69:13), "good" (Psalm 69:16), "great above the heavens" (Psalm 108:4), and which "endures for ever" (Psalm 107:1). The New Testament identifies the coming of Christ as the gift of God's love.

> For God so loved the world that he gave his only Son, that whoever believes in him should not perish but have eternal life. For God sent the Son into the world, not to condemn the world, but that the world might be saved through him.
> —John 3:16–17

E. M. Good says that love of God "is not the emotional or intellectual imposition of a favorable viewpoint upon an object of love" ("Love in the Old Testament" in *The Interpreter's Dictionary of the Bible*). It is not the sentimental affection that is sometimes associated with the word *love*. The biblical picture of divine love, according to G. Johnston, is of "an active benevolence that will go to any length to do good to the beloved object and to secure its well-being." It is a relationship of "devotion, loyalty, intimate knowledge, and responsibility" ("Love in the New Testament" in *The Interpreter's Dictionary of the Bible*). God's love is expressed in God's care for the whole creation.

In the Old Testament, God's gift of law was understood to be an expression of God's care for the people. The law regulated and protected relationships in the community. Righteousness was understood not as simple obedience to the law but as doing those things that preserved the peace and wholeness of that community. One of the most popular witnesses in the Old Testament to the nature of God is the word *righteousness*, for God's actions were perceived as oriented to the well-being of the whole community.

Jesus expands this understanding of God's love by repeatedly addressing God as *Father.* God, says Jesus, cares for the creation, clothing the grass and feeding the ravens, and providing for the human creatures as well (Luke 12:22–31). Jesus revealed this love in his life of concern and care for others. The depth of this love is made known in the cross.

Paul says that "God's love has been poured into our hearts through the Holy Spirit which has been given to us" (Rom. 5:5). And he makes one of the great affirmations of Christian faith in this love in his letter to the Romans:

> For I am sure that neither death, nor life, nor angels, nor principalities, nor things present, nor things to come, nor powers, nor height, nor depth, nor anything else in all creation, will be able to separate us from the love of God in Christ Jesus our Lord.
> —Romans 8:38–39

One of the unique characteristics of Christian prayer is that it is communication with a divine being whose nature is love. In their book *Process Theology: An Introductory Exposition,* John Cobb and David Griffin point out that this love can be thought of in two ways: as creative love and as responsive love. In fact, all of the ways God is experienced in the Christian tradition can be understood as an expression of creative-responsive love.

As creative love, God calls the world to realize the ideal possibilities which are God's will for the world. Jean-Pierre De Caussade speaks of "God's treasury" which is unlocked by faith. In God's treasury are all the possibilities for the maximum well-being of the creation. A variety of words are used to describe what God wills for us: *shalom,* strength of beauty, peace, complete fulfillment, the kingdom of God. God is not a great cosmic Santa Claus to whom we come with a list or the "vending machine in the sky" with handles for all the goodies we might want. But God does desire that we realize the potentiality of each moment of our existence. God calls us forward into a future of possibility. God confronts us in every moment where we are with what is possible for us.

Alfred North Whitehead, writing in *Process and Reality,* describes God as "the poet of the world, with tender patience leading it by his vision of truth, beauty, and goodness." God goes before us with the ideal possibilities for us, seeking to lure us on. These possibilities are geared to where we are in each

35

moment. The decisions we have made in the past determine our starting place in creating the present. But the past does not determine completely what our present is or what our future shall be. God is actively present with us, presenting us with new possibilities for our unique place in life. We are free to respond to God's "call forward." We cannot escape our past or change it, but we do not have to be captives of the past. Because of God's activity in us and among us, there can be progress in the world.

In a hymn based on Psalm 8, Curtis Beach describes this sense of being called into the future by God's creative love envisioning possibilities for us.

> O how wondrous, O how glorious
> Is thy name in every land!
> Thou whose purpose moves before us
> Toward the goal that thou has planned.
>
> 'Tis thy will our hearts are seeking,
> Conscious of our human need.
> Spirit in our spirit speaking,
> Make us thine, O God, indeed!

The power which God uses in calling us forward is the power of persuasion or attraction. Power is sometimes exercised by pushing, forcing, altering by fiat. Power is sometimes exercised by attraction, influence, like a magnet. In the hymn "Sing Praise to God Who Reigns Above," Johann Schütz wrote, "As with a mother's tender hand, [God] lead's his own, his chosen band." This is the kind of power we witness in the life of Christ who came humbly, lived without the signs and symbols of coercive power, resisted in the desert the temptation to seek the power of force, and yet had tremendous power to attract and to call forth the best in people. In the face of the dominating, brute force of the Roman empire and the Jewish religious establishment of his time, he suffered the crucifixion. Yet the force of love that dwelt in Christ has ultimately prevailed. God works in the world through the persuasive power of love.

The church sings its faith in God's call forward. With hymnist William Williams, we sing, "Guide me, O thou great Jehovah,/ Pilgrim through this barren land." And in Joseph H. Gilmore's words, "He leadeth me, he leadeth me,/By his own hand he leadeth me."

God may be experienced not only as creative love, but also as

36

responsive love. We do not take advantage of all of the possibilities that God offers to us. In each moment, we have not only the influence of the past and the call of God into the future. We have our own free will. What we become is the result of what we choose to do with what we are given. We make mistakes. We fail. We choose destructive rather than constructive patterns of behavior. Sometimes we get ourselves into trouble. Sometimes forces and factors beyond our control cause us pain and suffering. Things don't go smoothly, accidents occur, disease develops, life gets complicated. God is present with us as responsive love.

> O Love divine that stooped to share
> Our sharpest pang, our bitterest tear,
> On thee we cast each earthborn care;
> We smile at pain while thou art near.
> —Oliver Wendell Holmes

One of the images of God that blocks prayer is the image of the stern judge or divine criticizing parent waiting to catch us in disobedience in order to punish us severely. Such images may originate in childhood, when we hear threats that God will punish us if we misbehave. Such images lurking in the back of an adult mind need to be exorcised before prayer can become a positive opportunity.

One of the most beautiful pictures of the nature of God is given in the parable of the prodigal son. A central figure in the parable is the forgiving father who runs to welcome the child who has wasted all that he has been given. The father calls for an extravagant celebration because the prodigal has seen the errors of his ways and has come back to the relationship of the family. The father bestows on his son new gifts of grace. God's love is expressed in forgiveness which is offered in the face of our rejection of God and our wandering ways.

God's offer of forgiveness is one of the central affirmations of the Christian faith. The scriptures testify to it:

> The Lord is merciful and gracious,
> slow to anger and abounding in steadfast love.
> He will not always chide,
> nor will he keep his anger forever.
> He does not deal with us according to our sins,
> nor requite us according to our iniquities.
> For as the heavens are high above the earth,

so great is his steadfast love toward those who fear him;
as far as the east is from the west,
so far does he remove our transgressions from us.
As a father pities his children,
so the Lord pities those who fear him.
For he knows our frame; he remembers that we are dust.
    —Psalm 103:8–14

The great creeds of the church witness to it. In the Apostles' Creed, we say, "I believe in . . . the forgiveness of sins." The church sings its faith in forgiveness. In Charles Wesley's moving hymn, "O For a Thousand Tongues to Sing," we are assured that "He breaks the power of canceled sin, He sets the prisoner free." And our liturgy reflects it:

Almighty God, our heavenly Father, who of thy great mercy hast promised forgiveness of sins to all them that with hearty repentance and true faith turn to thee: Have mercy upon us; pardon and deliver us from all our sins; confirm and strengthen us in all goodness; and bring us to everlasting life; through Jesus Christ our Lord. Amen
    —From "The Order for the Administration of the Sacrament of The Lord's Supper or Holy Communion" in *The Book of Hymns*

God's forgiveness can be experienced in two ways. God accepts us just as we are and in every moment offers to us new possibilities appropriate to where we are. No matter what we have done or have omitted doing, God is still with us, leading us with creative love. We are "judged" by God in the sense that God "can give us only what we will receive" (*God and the World* by John Cobb). Those who are responsive to God are able to receive increasingly rich challenges, while those who are unresponsive have fewer opportunities. But wherever we are, God is there with us in that place.

God's forgiveness can also be experienced in what God does with our past. The past cannot be erased. But God takes the past into the divine being. The good, the bad, and the indifferent experiences of the world are taken into God's own being as they become part of the past. There all of the values are synthesized and preserved. In *Process and Reality*, Whitehead concludes that God is able to use "what in the temporal world is mere wreckage."

The beautiful persian rugs that are famous around the world

are made on a frame with a group of boys on one side who feed threads through to an artist who sits on the other side giving directions. If one of the boys makes a mistake, the artist may change the design to compensate for the error. The error is not erased, but instead it becomes part of a new design created to take it into account and still create a thing of beauty. This is a parable of God's forgiveness.

Our failure and sin are not without cost to God. The cross of Christ, the central symbol of Christianity, is the symbol of God's suffering for our sin. God has suffered, and God continues to suffer for and with us. Alfred North Whitehead describes God as "the great companion—the fellow-sufferer who understands" (*Process and Reality*).

God is affected by what we do. This may be a shocking idea for some people. Our ways of thinking about God have been influenced by Greek philosophy as well as by the scriptures. The idea that God is unchangeable has come into our heritage from Greek philosophy. The God of responsive love is a God who is affected by what we do.

In the Old Testament there is the story of Abraham bargaining with God to save the city of Sodom. God wants to destroy the city because of the evil that exists in it. Abraham convinces God to spare it for the sake of the righteous people who live there (Gen. 18:20–33). God's mind is also changed about destroying Ninevah (Jonah 3:10). It is both reasonable and Christian to believe that God is affected by us.

This reponsive love of God provides the ground of meaning for our existence. Our simplest actions, our most private thoughts, can matter to us because they matter to God. They make an everlasting contribution to the world as preserved in God. No matter what happens in the future, even if our accomplishments seem to add up to nothing, our lives are meaningful because what we do matters to God. This includes our prayers.

Like the Hebrews whose conceptions of God's presence grew from the pillars of cloud and fire to the tent to the ark to the dynasty, our concepts are also inadequate to the reality of God. All of our language about God is necessarily symbolic. We can speak of God as father, as mother, as the ground of being, as the fellow-sufferer who understands, as the one who calls. But these are metaphors. If we make idols of any of our metaphors, we lock ourselves into one stage of spiritual growth. Assuming that we know more than we know may be necessary to some extent in the life of faith. However, premature finality in describing God can choke and smother true growth in the life of the spirit. Our pilgrimage of faith involves a dynamic relationship with God in which our limited and inadequate metaphors are in the process of being replaced by images that penetrate more deeply into the reality of God. The worship of God, says Alfred North Whitehead, is an "adventure of the spirit" (*Science and the Modern World*).

QUESTIONS FOR REFLECTION AND DISCUSSION

1. What were your ideas about God when you were a child?
2. Which of these ideas do you still believe or hold in your feelings in spite of your adult beliefs?
3. What do you need to believe about God before you can begin to pray?
4. What experiences in your life have caused you to expand your concept of God?
5. At what point in reading the material on thinking about God did you experience the most discomfort or resistance?
6. At any point, did you find yourself agreeing with your "heart," your feelings, as well as with your mind?
7. What questions about your own concepts of God remain unanswered?

How Can *You* Think about God?

Several ways of thinking about God have been described in Session One. How does your image of God compare? Check the columns as indicated and use the space at the bottom of the sheet to add ways you would describe God not discussed in this material.

HOW CAN WE THINK ABOUT GOD?

	Agree	Disagree	Not Sure
1. God is a person.			
2. God is more than personal.			
3. God is spirit.			
4. God is male.			
5. God is masculine.			
6. God is in heaven.			
7. God is immediately present to every place.			
8. God is present with us in every moment.			
9. God knows us better than we know ourselves.			
10. God is too busy for the ordinary cares and details of our lives.			
11. Truth can only be known from God's perspective.			
12. God is beyond the creation as well as within the creation.			
13. God is the ground of our unity with the rest of the creation.			
14. God is love.			
15. God's love is an active benevolence that will go to any length to do good to the beloved object and to secure its well-being.			
16. God's love is poured into our hearts by the Holy Spirit.			
17. God offers us ideal possibilities for our existence.			
18. God uses the power of persuasion.			
19. God suffers with us.			
20. God judges us.			
21. God is like a critical parent.			
22. God forgives us.			
23. God is able to use what in the temporal world is mere wreckage.			
24. God is affected by what we do.			
25. All of our metaphors for God are inadequate.			
26.			
27.			
28.			

41

Look again at the items you have checked. Star the ones that make it possible for you to pray. Put an X by those that block you in prayer. You may want to share your reactions and additions to this list with the person or group sharing this study with you.

If there are X's on the list that bother you, perhaps you could talk about these with your group, or your pastor, or a Christian friend. Check the bibliography for additional reading resources.

A GUIDE FOR DAILY PRAYER: TWO

Preparation and Centering

Be still, and know that I am God.
—Psalm 46:10

They who wait for the Lord shall renew their strength.
—Isaiah 40:31

Praise and Adoration

O God, you are my God, and I long for you.
My whole being desires you;
like a dry, worn-out, and waterless land, my soul is thirsty
for you.
Let me see you in the sanctuary; let me see how mighty and
glorious you are.
Your constant love is better than life itself, and so I will
praise you.
I will give you thanks as long as I live.
My soul will feast and be satisfied, and I will sing glad
songs of praise to you.
—Psalm 63:1–5 (TEV)

Confession

O God, as I come to worship you, I am aware of my own
sin. In preparation for listening for your word to me in this
day, I confess my need for your forgiveness. I have sinned
against you in thought, word and deed, by what I have done
and by what I have left undone. I have not loved you with
all of my heart. I have not loved my neighbor as myself. I
am truly sorry and I humbly repent.
—Adapted from the *Book of Common Prayer*

43

Forgive me through Jesus Christ. In the power of the Holy Spirit, strengthen me in goodness and keep me in eternal life.

Meditative Reading of Scripture

Day One—Matthew 6:9–13
Day Two—1 Samuel 1:1–2:11
Day Three—Psalm 51:1–12
Day Four—Ephesians 3:14–19
Day Five—Matthew 6:1–8
Day Six—John 4:7–15
Day Seven—Jeremiah 31:31–34

Insights from the scriptures:

Petitions

With Hannah, O God, I pour out my troubles before you and share with you the pain in my life. I ask you for what I need.

With the psalmist, I pray for the joy that comes from your salvation.

With Paul, I pray for power through your Spirit to be strong in my inner being.

With the disciples, I ask you to teach me how to pray.

Intercessions

I pray for the leaders of my government. May they do justice, love mercy, and walk in the way of truth.

I pray for the poor. May they be remembered and their needs be met out of your bounty as we learn to save and to share.

I pray for those in pain or distress. Grant to them courage, relief and refreshment, and the comfort of your sustaining presence. I remember especially. . . .

I pray for my enemies. May the tangled relationships be unraveled, and the wounds healed, and through the mystery of your grace may we become friends. I pray for. . . .

Fulfill my prayers as may be best for those for whom I have prayed.

Thanksgiving

Gracious God, I am thankful for all of your goodness to me, and to all that you have made. I thank you for creating, preserving, and blessing my life. I thank you for the gift of salvation in Jesus Christ, for the ways in which you continue to sustain and guide me in every day, and for the hope you make possible. Make me so aware of your gifts that I may respond not only with my lips in praise and thanksgiving, but also with my life in holy living and dedicated service to you.
—Adapted from the *Book of Common Prayer*

Dedication

Day by day,
Dear Lord, of thee three things I pray:
To see thee more clearly,
Love thee more dearly.
Follow thee more nearly.
Day by day.
Amen.
—Richard of Chichester

Silence

Benediction

May the God of hope fill us with all joy and peace in believing through the power of the Holy Spirit. Amen.
—*Book of Common Prayer*

SESSION THREE: *How Can We Think about Prayer?*

Prayer is a "mysterious linking of the human and the Divine ... an incomprehensible wonder, a miracle of miracles," says Friedrich Heiler in his book *Prayer*. It is a living communion between human beings and God, the bringing of our finite spirits into direct touch with the infinite spirit of God in a conscious and intentional way. This linking is made possible by God's initiative, by the working of the Spirit within us.

In this century we have experienced many marvelous developments in communication. We can pick up a telephone and talk directly to someone on the other side of the globe. The conversation flows back and forth almost as if we were in the same room. Human beings soar through space to the moon and carry on conversations with their colleagues back on earth with almost instantaneous communication. We see what is going on in other parts of the world televised live into our homes via satellite. It seems like a miracle.

Our ancestors in faith have experienced communication between the human spirit and God's spirit for thousands of years. This "direct touch" has been taken for granted as far back in history as our biblical record goes. Yet it, too, remains a source of wonder and amazement. It is to this miracle of miracles that we attempt now to give some careful thought. Assuming what has already been said about God, how can we think about prayer?

Prayer as Openness

A key word in thinking about prayer is openness. God is always present with us, relating to us in every moment of our lives as creative and responsive love. But we are free to choose either to ignore or to give attention to that presence. Prayer is the act of being intentionally open to God.

Many persons and things are present to us every day. We are bombarded by an incredible number of messages and bits of information in the course of a day. There is no way that we could be consciously and intentionally open to all of them. We have to screen out many of the signals that come to us through our senses of sight, hearing, smell, taste, and touch. We are not always free to choose what our environment will be, either internally or externally. But we do have some freedom of choice in deciding what our response to that environment will be. If I am walking in a beautiful park on a warm, spring day, I can choose to listen for bird songs and look for birds. Or I can choose to enjoy the beauty of color in the new leaves and the flowers against the darker green of the grass and the blue of the sky. Or I can be absorbed in analyzing a painful disagreement with someone important to me and not be consciously aware of the birds or the colors at all. Likewise, in a crowded restaurant, it is possible for me to keep up with a boring conversation at my table while listening in on a more interesting conversation at the next table! We do have power in deciding to what we will consciously pay attention.

God is a constant part of our environment. We can ignore that presence. We also can open ourselves to communion with that presence. To do so is to pray. Prayer involves two kinds of openness: openness *to* God and openness *with* God.

Some of the leaders of the Christian church in the second and third centuries after Christ used the Greek word *homilia* or its root form *homilein* for prayer. This word can mean being or living together, conversing or dealing with one another, encountering, being friends. Prayer is in some ways like a human social relationship or friendship. In friendship, we are open *to* the other person. We listen, respect, and try to understand the other person. We try to see things from her or his perspective. We are also open *with* a friend. We share ourselves honestly. We reveal what it is like to be who we are. We tell what is going on in our world. In prayer we are open to who God is and what God's truth and purposes are. And we tell God who we are and what we need and desire.

Jesus gave his disciples a model for prayer that reflected this two-dimensional openness. In the Lord's Prayer, there are six major petitions. In the first three, attention is focused on God.

> Our Father who art in heaven,
> Hallowed be thy name.
> Thy kingdom come,
> Thy will be done,
> On earth as it is in heaven.
> —Matthew 6:9–10

The one who prays is open to who God is, expresses respect for God's being, and shares in wanting what God wants for the world. The prayer begins with a response *to* God from the mind, the emotions, and the will of the one who prays. The second three petitions make known the requests of the disciples who pray.

> Give us this day our daily bread;
> And forgive us our debts,
> As we also have forgiven our debtors;
> And lead us not into temptation,
> But deliver us from evil.
> —Matthew 6:11–13

Our physical needs, our relationships, the struggles of our existence—the whole of our life is appropriately shared openly with God.

Perhaps our thinking about prayer can be helped by a more careful look at the two sides of our participation in this "mysterious linking" called prayer.

Openness to God

Prayer has been described as a time exposure of the soul to God. When film is exposed it is changed. It reflects that to which it has been exposed. When we become open to God in prayer, we grant God the power to shape and transform us in the relationship. John Cobb speaks of the divine "field of force." When we open ourselves to God in prayer, we put ourselves in that field of force. Like metal filings in the force field of a

49

powerful magnet, we will find ourselves attracted and creatively transformed. When we open ourselves to God, we give power to God's call forward to the vast possibilities that God offers to us.

A popular old gospel hymn by Annie S. Hawks expresses this openness *to* God:

> I need thee every hour
> Teach me thy will;
> And thy rich promises
> In me fulfill.

Peter Annet is quoted as saying that praying people are "like sailors who have cast anchor on a rock, and who imagine they are pulling the rock to themselves, when they are really pulling themselves to the rock" (*The Meaning of Prayer* by Harry Emerson Fosdick). Christlikeness, or Christian maturity, is the goal toward which we will be drawn if we open ourselves to God in prayer. Another of Samuel Longfellow's hymns invites this transformation.

> Holy Spirit, Truth divine,
> Dawn upon this soul of mine;
> Word of God and inward light,
> Wake my spirit, clear my sight.
>
> Holy Spirit, Love divine,
> Glow within this heart of mine;
> Kindle every high desire;
> Perish self in thy pure fire.
>
> Holy Spirit, Power divine,
> Fill and nerve this will of mine;
> By thee may I strongly live,
> Bravely bear and nobly strive.
>
> Holy Spirit, Right divine,
> King within my conscience reign;
> Be my Lord, and I shall be
> Firmly bound, forever free.

When we open ourselves to God in prayer, we leave our private, enclosed worlds and enter a broader, shared world. We lift our eyes from our limited self-interest to look at reality from the perspective of God. Our inner world becomes connected to universality.

HOW CAN WE THINK ABOUT PRAYER?

When we open ourselves to God in prayer, we make a way for the work of God's creative love in our lives. In "Opening" from *Diary of Daily Prayer*, Barry Shepherd speaks of being open to God.

> Lord, teach me to be open, and receptive in my praying.
> So often, when I pray,
> the only thing that is open is my mouth.
> My eyes are shut tight,
> and with them my mind and my heart.
> Lord, teach me to be open to the leading of your Spirit
> as I pray.
>
> In these times of concern for dialog between persons,
> I have allowed my praying to degenerate
> into a tedious monolog
> in which I do all the talking
> and you do all the listening.
> Yet it is written:
> "Be still, and know that I am God."
> And again:
> "In quietness and in trust shall be your strength."
>
> So teach me, Father,
> that prayer is both a matter of speaking,
> and of silence.
> Draw especially close now
> as I set a few minutes aside
> to wait in silence,
> and listen expectantly for your Word:
> your judgment on my sin,
> your forgiveness in Jesus my Lord,
> your response to my requests,
> your call to my readiness.
>
> Let me learn again, Lord,
> the prayer of your servant Samuel:
> "Speak, Lord, for your servant hears."
> And let me make this prayer my own
> tonight and always.

Openness with God

Harry Emerson Fosdick, in his popular book, *The Meaning of Prayer*, points out that prayer is the "personal appropriation of this faith that God cares for each of us. . . . Belief by itself is a map of the unvisited land of God's care; prayer is actually traveling the country." Prayer is an expression of faith in God's responsive love as well.

The scriptures contain an abundance of models of honest, open self-revelation in prayer. Ezra leads his people in confession:

> O my God, I am ashamed and blush to lift my face to thee, my God, for our iniquities have risen higher than our heads, and our guilt has mounted up to the heavens.
> —Ezra 9:6

Jeremiah complains about the way God is treating him. He accuses God of being to him "like a deceitful brook, like waters that fail" (Jer. 15:18). Jonah expresses his anger to God in a prayer to die (Jon. 4:1–3). The Psalms are full of expressions of the full range of human conditions shared with God in rich detail and extravagant imagery.

> For evils have encompassed me without number;
> my iniquities have overtaken me, till I cannot see;
> they are more than the hairs of my head;
> my heart fails me.
> —Psalm 40:12

> Be gracious to me, O Lord, for I am in distress;
> my eye is wasted from grief,
> my soul and my body also.
> For my life is spent with sorrow,
> and my years with sighing.
> —Psalm 31:9–10

> My soul longs, yea, faints
> for the courts of the Lord;
> my heart and flesh sing for joy
> to the living God.
> —Psalm 84:2

Personal needs and desires are expressed, and there is intercession for other people in need. There are prayers to be saved from one's problems and enemies. There are prayers for healing of both mental and physical ills. Sometimes there is a kind of struggle of wills between the human desire and the divine purpose. Self-revelation becomes encounter and confrontation. Prayer in the Bible, on occasion, is more honest than polite.

The openness with God in scripture is based on the assumption that not only are we affected by God in prayer, but that our prayers make a difference to God. In the New Testament, the author of James says, "The prayer of a righteous man has great power in its effects" (James 5:16). Since the prayer is directed to God, one assumes that the prayer affects God.

One of the striking and consistent characteristics of biblical prayer is its honesty. One of the most serious blocks to prayer is dishonesty, or role-playing with God. All of us play roles. We may fill the role of secretary to a boss, dentist to a patient, parent to a child, spouse to a husband or wife. And all of us wear masks. They are necessary in our social relationships. But in prayer, roles can be abandoned and masks put aside. God knows our true selves better than we even know ourselves. We do not need to play the saint with God, saying all of the right things. We do not need to pretend or hide. Prayer is a matter of honest communication between a genuine "I" and a "Thou" who knows us intimately, loves us unconditionally (even when we role-play!), and hears us in a way that makes a difference.

Prayer as such open and honest communication is often described as a matter of the heart. Our deepest concerns are appropriately revealed to God in prayer.

The Heart as the Locus of Prayer

There is a second way in which prayer may be thought of as a matter of the heart. R. C. Denton, writing in *The Interpreters Dictionary of the Bible*, notes that the "heart" is "the central and unifying organ of personal life"—the core of our being. In *Contemplative Prayer*, Thomas Merton defines the heart as "the root and source of all one's own inner truth." It is the place where we most are who we are, where we know who we are.

In Hebrew thought as reflected in the scriptures, this was the part of the human being through which contact was made with the divine. Human-divine transactions took place in the heart. God worked there to transform character.

> But this is the covenant which I will make with the house of Israel after those days, says the Lord: I will put my law within them, and I will write it upon their hearts; and I will be their God, and they shall be my people.
> —Jeremiah 31:33

Create in me a clean heart, O God, and put a new and right spirit within me.
    —Psalm 51:10

God's love has been poured into our hearts through the Holy Spirit which has been given to us.
    —Romans 5:5

That Christ may dwell in your hearts through faith.
    —Ephesians 3:17

Since the heart or core of our being is where God meets us and works with us, then the heart is the place where prayer occurs.

Our twentieth-century minds are more used to locating the center of personality in the brain. We talk about the rational, analytical functions of the left brain, and the emotional, intuitive functions of the right brain. To translate the idea of the heart as the center of our personality, it is probably necessary to think of the whole brain, not only the right and left, but the conscious and subconscious as well.

The Eastern Orthodox branch of the church has a tradition of speaking of three interpenetrating levels of prayer: the prayer of the lips, the prayer of the mind, and the prayer of the heart, or of the mind in the heart. Prayer may be a matter of the lips, but it needs to include also the mind and the center of our being, the place where we most are who we are.

In prayer, one turns inward to find God. One turns one's attention inward to what the Quaker Thomas Kelly, writing in *A Testament of Devotion*, calls the "sanctuary of the soul." Saint Teresa of Avila repeatedly returned to this theme in her spiritual direction. "The Lord is within us," she said in *The Way of Perfection*. "The soul collects together all the faculties and enters within itself to be with its God." This is not just the perception of the Quakers and the saints. Even the great prophet of the social gospel, Walter Rauschenbusch, witnessed to this experience of finding God in the center of his being in his poem "The Little Gate to God."

> In the castle of my soul
> Is a little garden gate,
> Whereat, when I enter
> I am in the presence of God.

HOW CAN WE THINK ABOUT PRAYER?

In a moment, in the turning of a thought,
I am where God is,
That is a fact.

This is not to say that we possess God or that all of God is inside us. Rather it is to say that God is present in the center of our being and that we can encounter the divine spirit there. Harry Emerson Fosdick, with his genius for analogy, gives a picture of how God is close to us and yet far beyond.

Each time I visit my island off the coast of Maine, I fall in love with the sea again. Now I don't know all of the sea—wide areas of it are unknown to me—but I know the sea. It has a near range. It washes my island. I can sit beside it . . . and sail over it, and be sung to sleep by the music of it. God is like that. He is so great in His vastness that we can only think of him in symbolic terms, but he has a near range.
—From *Breakaway* by Mark Link

Forms of Prayer

Communion with God in prayer takes many forms in the Christian tradition. Words and verbal forms of communication are used in most public worship, although the Society of Friends, or Quakers, are well known for their silent meetings. Prayers in public worship may be strictly prescribed in a standard liturgy, written fresh for each service of worship, or created spontaneously in the service, or a combination of these forms depending on the traditions and customs of a worshiping community. Some people pray in tongues, others chant, or use mantras. Prayers can be sung. But prayer without words is possible too. Prayer can take the form of thought or creative visualization or the more passive quiet contemplation. In individual prayer, the beginner may find the use of words necessary. As with a new acquaintance, silence may be awkward. Even words may be awkward. As he said in *The Soul of Prayer*, P. T. Forsyth finds that "words fail us in prayer oftener than anywhere else." But as the relationship between God and the person in prayer develops and matures, the number of words may decline. As it is possible to simply be together in silence with an intimate friend, so it is possible to be silent in prayer.

Prayer is not a special privilege reserved for people who are good with words. How perfectly or imperfectly a person speaks is unimportant in personal prayer. God can hear the profound meanings in our simplest words and behind them knows our minds—and hearts!

The story is told of a simple peasant who regularly spent an hour each day sitting in the front row of a small Catholic chapel in his town. One day the priest met him as he left and made so bold as to ask him what he did each day in the chapel. He pointed to the crucifix hanging over the altar before which he sat and said, "I just look at him and he looks at me."

As prayer can be both verbal and nonverbal, it can also be both public and private, or corporate and individual. In fact, it is important for the prayer life of the Christian to have both. We are to pray both in our room with the door shut, where our Father who "sees in secret" (Matt. 6:6) will reward us, and in groups gathered together in Christ's name where his presence is in the midst of us (Matt. 18:20).

Kenneth Leech uses the words *solitude* and *solidarity* to describe these two settings for prayer, and he points out that they are "inseparably linked." Each is complementary to the other. As Christians we are called to join with the church in common worship and prayer. We need to share in listening for God's word to the church and to join in the prayers of the community. We need prayer in solidarity with our Christian brothers and sisters. There, as Evelyn Underhill points out, "we are released from a narrow selfish outlook on the universe by a common act of worship" (*Collected Papers of Evelyn Underhill*). But public worship can become empty ritual or impersonal form. Prayer in solitude can help sensitize the worshiper to the significance of the liturgy and increase personal involvement in what happens there. Prayer in solitude provides the opportunity for interacting with God about the unique business of our own lives. But private prayer needs the guidance and inspiration of common prayer. A person who prays only alone is in danger of drifting into individualistic piety that is something other than Christian faith. Participation in both public and private prayer is essential for wholeness in the experience of Christian prayer.

Whether we pray in the privacy of our room or in community, we are praying as the church. We may pray in solitude but not in isolation. For those who pray in Christ's name, pray as a part of God's people in Christ. In that sense, all prayer, even the prayer of the hermit in the desert or the invalid in the nursing home can be corporate prayer.

There is no such thing as a purely private relationship between a single human being and the "person" of God, for we come as part of Christ's church. We encounter in God our interconnectedness with all that is.

Prayer in the Vision of God

Finally, it is important to note the place of prayer in the vision or purpose of God. In *Reality and Prayer*, John Magee calls prayer as a relationship of communion with God "the Kingdom in embryo." Jesus' summary of the law in the great commandment begins with the commandment to love God with our whole being (Matt. 22:37). A conscious, intentional relationship with God in prayer is one of the ways this love is expressed and nurtured. Even in our simplest and most elementary prayers, we are doing the will of God.

Prayer is one means of grace. God can work in our lives through the prayer relationship in healing, whole-making, saving ways. Prayer is not a human enterprise. God comes to us. God's spirit works in us, offering this mysterious linking of the divine Spirit with our spirits, making possible this communion of Heart with heart. Our part is but to respond to the divine gift. This communion is one of the ways we are called forward to our full humanity and invited to be what Peter calls "partakers of the divine nature (2 Pet. 1:4).

Quoting Dr. Fosdick in *The Meaning of Prayer* once again; "The Gospel offers a great privilege; prayer appropriates it."

QUESTIONS FOR REFLECTION AND DISCUSSION

1. Where do you locate the core of your personhood? Can you think of God as present and communicating with you there?
2. Think back to times when you were aware of praying from your heart. What form did the prayer take? Was it verbal or nonverbal, public or private?
3. In what ways have you experienced prayer as healing, whole-making, saving?
4. When have you been open *to* God? When have you been open *with* God?

A GUIDE FOR DAILY PRAYER: THREE

Preparation and Centering

For God alone my soul waits in silence.
—Psalm 62:5

You have been raised to life with Christ; so set your heart
on the things that have been revealed in him.
—Colossians 3:1 (AP)

Praise and Adoration

My soul praises you, O God!
With all my being, I praise your holy name!
I will not forget all of your benefits,
You will forgive all of my guilt and heal all of my suffering,
You rescue me from the pit of death
and surround me with love and mercy.
You fill my life with good things,
You judge in favor of the oppressed,
You do not punish us as we deserve,
Your goodness endures to all generations.
My soul praises you, O God!
—Psalm 103:1–18 (AP)

Confession

All have sinned and fallen short of your glory. This is true for
me.

Forgive my sins, O God. Do not remember my wrongs any more. Write your will upon my heart and preserve me among your people.

Meditative Reading of Scripture

Day One—Psalm 8
Day Two—Psalm 103:1–5
Day Three—Psalm 103:6–14
Day Four—Luke 1:46–55
Day Five—Luke 18:1–17
Day Six—Matthew 7:7–11
Day Seven—Isaiah 40:27–31

Insights from the scriptures:

Petitions

In response to your invitation, I share my troubles, my worries, my deepest needs with you.

Open my mind to the ideas, possibilities, relationships, understandings that are your will for me. Lift my vision beyond the boundaries of this world to the horizons of your new possibilities.

Help me to root out of my life discrimination against those who are different or in the minority.

Save me from the worship of idols—money, success, power, relevance, popularity, another person.

I pray for. . . .

Intercessions

I pray for your church. May all who have been baptized into its fellowship be filled with your spirit and made perfect in love and good works. I pray especially for. . . .

I pray for my family. Teach us to weave those fragile threads of gentle love which eventually combine to create a cable of trust and affection binding us together. I pray today especially for. . . .

I pray for those who have experienced loss. Surround them with your love, comfort them with your presence and give them your peace. I make this prayer especially for. . . .

I pray for the hungry and homeless of this world. Help us to find ways to end hunger and war on this planet.

I pray for. . . .

You know what we need before we ask. You know our needs better than we know them ourselves. Grant those things that meet our true needs and that fit in with your will for our lives.

Thanksgiving

Eternal Spirit, your never-falling grace is the source of all hope and the lure that tugs me in the direction of all good things. Thank you for the goodness that I do not deserve and cannot earn or repay. Today I am especially thankful for. . . .

Dedication

God be in my head, and in my understanding;
God be in mine eyes, and in my looking;
God be in my mouth, and in my speaking;
God be in my heart, and in my thinking;
God be at mine end, and at my departing.
—*Sarum Primer*, 1558

Silence

Benediction

Grant, O God, that I may both perceive the things I ought to do and have the grace and power to do them. Amen.

SESSION FOUR: *How Can We Pray?*

Preparation and Centering

"Be still and know that I am God," an admonition from the Psalms (46:10), gives us a good starting place for prayer. "Be still?" responds a chorus of voices. "With all I have to do? That may have been possible for a wandering people camping in the desert at night or for village folk in ancient Palestine. Life was simpler in those days. But in the twentieth-century rat race, that's easier said than done!"

In *Rufus Jones Speaks to Our Time*, the Quaker writer points to the problem of finding time to be still as a major block to the kind of prayer that makes a difference.

> Hush, waiting, meditation, concentration of spirit, are just the reverse of our busy, driving, modern temper. The person who meditates, we are apt to think, will lose an opportunity to do something; while he muses, the procession will go on and leave him behind.

Stillness is not essential to prayer. We can pray in the middle of noise and confusion. But the experience of the church across the centuries has been that "being still" is helpful in enhancing awareness of the presence of God. Finding or making time to pray is a first and major step.

Regular participation in congregational worship provides a disciplined structure for prayer and gives a framework in which the personal devotional life can be set. A small group in which people share the prayer experience and hold each other accountable for personal spiritual disciplines can provide valuable support and encouragement. The consistent use of a devotional periodical at a set time each day is a pattern followed by millions of people. Setting the time and place for prayer is a personal matter and, not surprisingly, for many people this is a major hurdle.

Whatever the time and place of prayer, it is usually a good idea to spend the first few minutes in collecting the mind, relaxing the body, and surrendering the spirit to openness in prayer. The purpose of being still is in order to know that God is God, to be aware of God's presence with us.

Rufus Jones tells a story of a group of children on an island just off the New England coast. A visitor decided to have a summer Sunday School for the children. The island was so tiny that the ocean could be seen from every part of it. The children could hear the sound of the surf from the time they woke in the morning until they went to sleep at night. They could smell the salty sea air with every breath. Most of the protein in their diet came from the ocean. They had sailed across its surface in their father's boats, and they had played in its waves on the beaches. The teacher gathered the children for the first lesson. Beginning with the familiar, the teacher asked, "How many of you have seen the Atlantic Ocean?" The children did not respond. They looked at the teacher blankly, not knowing what he was talking about. The Atlantic Ocean was their constant environment, but nobody had ever named it or interpreted it to them (*Rufus Jones Speaks to Our Time*).

This is a parable of our life, says Jones. God is a constant part of our environment. Prayer begins with conscious openness to that presence. It is as if we are sharing a room or a car with someone else. Our attention may be on other things, but we suddenly realize the other is there. "Oh yes, you are here too!" And communication with that other then begins to be the center of our attention. Because God is present with us as spirit rather than as another body, being in touch with our own spirit (centering, being quiet) helps us to be aware, "Oh yes, you are here too!"

Praise and Adoration

The traditional starting place for our response to the presence of God is praise or adoration. This is a crucial but frequently neglected part of prayer. Since our need for God is what drives us to prayer, it is easy to plunge immediately into the pouring out of our needs and desires. But the first petition of our model prayer is "Hallowed be thy name" with good reason. In praise and adoration, we acknowledge that we have some sense of who it is with whom we have communion, and we rejoice in and celebrate the relationship for itself.

James Sanders finds that sin in the Old Testament can be understood as the confusing of the gifts with the Giver. We make gods of the gifts of life and we forget the Giver. We worship the things God provides and neglect God, and we find our identity in hugging God's gifts rather than in the "awful" embrace of the Giver.

In praise and adoration, we respond to who God is with our rejoicing, by loving God with our heart, soul, mind, and strength. As in any other relationship, if this is taken for granted, something of indescribable importance is lost.

Expressing our praise to God may be awkward at first. We may find ourselves at a loss for words. Simple prose hardly seems adequate for the job. What do you say? Much of the praise and adoration in our tradition is in the form of poetry and song, found in the book of Psalms and in our hymnbooks. Our praise to God can be stimulated by reading and reflecting on the praise others have offered to God.

Our praise need not be eloquent. In *Letters to Malcolm: Chiefly on Prayer*, C. S. Lewis recounts a day when the language for praise was no longer a problem.

> You first taught me the great principle [of adoration], "Begin where you are." I had thought one had to start by summoning up what we believe about the goodness and greatness of God, by thinking about creation and redemption and "all the blessings of this life." You turned to the brook and once more splashed your burning face and hands in the little waterfall and said, "Why not begin with this?"
>
> And it worked. . . . That cushiony moss, that coldness and sound and dancing light were no doubt very minor blessings compared with "the means of grace and the hope of glory." But then they were manifest. So far as they were concerned, sight had replaced faith. They were not the hope of glory, they were an exposition of the glory itself.

Confession

A second way in which we can pray is confession. Isaiah reports on his vision of God in the temple as a young man. He sees God "high and lifted up" (Isa. 6:1). Around God is a chorus singing, "Holy, holy, holy is the Lord of hosts; the whole earth is full of his glory" (Isa. 6:3). Isaiah's response to this vision of a holy God is an overwhelming sense of his own unholiness: "And I said: 'Woe is me! For I am lost; for I am a man of unclean lips, and I dwell in the midst of a people of unclean lips; for my eyes have seen the King, the Lord of hosts!'" (Isa. 6:5)

The vision continues. One of the beings surrounding God comes to Isaiah with a burning coal "which he had taken with tongs from the altar. And he touched my [Isaiah's] mouth, and said: 'Behold, this has touched your lips; your guilt is taken away, and your sin forgiven'" (Isa. 6:6–7).

For centuries, people have seen in Isaiah's vision their own experience. In God's presence, their own imperfections have become keenly perceived. Confession to God in the spirit of repentance brings almost instantaneous awareness of God's forgiveness, with a liberating effect, a freeing for new life. Isaiah discovered himself to be now fit for God's service: "And I heard the voice of the Lord saying, 'Whom shall I send, and who will go for us?' Then I said, 'Here am I! Send me'" (Isa. 6:8). Echoes of Isaiah's experience can be heard in this early twentieth-century hymn by John Hunter:

> Dear Master, in whose life I see
> All that I would, but fail to be,
> Let thy clear light forever shine,
> To shame and guide this life of mine.
>
> Though what I dream and what I do
> In my weak days are always two,
> Help me, oppressed by things undone,
> O thou, whose deeds and dreams were one!

In God's presence we can come to know the truth about ourselves. If we are willing to be open and honest in prayer, to take off masks, to put aside roles, and reveal ourselves to the One who already knows us and yet loves us, then we can know the truth about ourselves.

Part of the truth about ourselves will be painful and unpleasant. In every life there will be unfinished business about which there may be some guilt. There will be behavior patterns that we regret. "All have sinned and fall short of the glory of God," says Paul (Rom. 3:23). And the author of 1 John asserts that: "If we say that we have no sin, we deceive ourselves, and the truth is not in us. If we confess our sins, he is faithful and just and will forgive our sins and cleanse us from all unrighteousness (1 John 1:8–9).

Mother Teresa of Calcutta, perhaps one of the most Christlike figures of our century, goes regularly to confession. A television interviewer, aware that Mother Teresa will probably be canonized as a saint by her church after her death, asks why. "I am a human being, and a sinner," she responds, "and so I need to go to confession regularly."

Twentieth-century psychologists have described a human defense against dealing honestly with the painful and unpleasant parts of our real selves. We create, they say, a kind of false self, an idealized image of ourself. Because we cannot escape the true self, we end up with two selves and a lack of integration in who we are.

God's transactions are with the real self. In confessional prayer, we can surrender the defensive ego and confess to being who we are. We might well come to confession with the words of a hymn by Clara H. Scott:

> Open my eyes, that I may see
> Glimpses of truth thou hast for me;
> Place in my hands the wonderful key
> That shall unclasp and set me free.
>
> Open my ears, that I may hear
> Voices of truth thou sendest clear;
> And while the wave-notes fall on my ear,
> Everything false will disappear.
>
> Silently now I wait for thee,
> Ready, my God thy will to see,
> Open my eyes, illumine me,
> Spirit divine!

Unfinished business from the past in the form of offenses and omissions for which we must assume some responsibility can burden us down in the present. Repressing feelings of guilt just makes a bad matter worse. Denying our share of the responsibility in an alienated relationship, our contribution to a destructive situation, is denying who we really are. Since God knows what we want to deny, such efforts to escape our own reality cut us off not only from ourselves but also from openness with God. In

HOW CAN WE PRAY?

Contemplative Prayer, Thomas Merton speaks of the "sense of loss, forsakenness and abandonment by God" that a person can experience when acting in contradiction to one's true condition.

The prayer of confession is a means to reconciliation. When we are willing to be open to our own truth, with the will to change our ways and to make amends, God's forgiveness can set us free. Remember the story of the prodigal son, and listen to the words of Psalm 103.

The Lord is merciful and gracious,
slow to anger and abounding in steadfast love.
He will not always chide,
nor will he keep his anger forever.
He does not deal with us according to our sins,
nor requite us according to our iniquities.
For as the heavens are high above the earth,
so great is his steadfast love toward those who
fear him;
as far as the east is from the west,
so far does he remove our transgressions from us.
    —Psalm 103:8–12

How shall we make our confession? Alcoholics Anonymous has discovered the central importance of confession in the process of recovering from alcoholism. In their "Twelve Steps" program, seven of the steps have to do with getting in touch with one's own reality through confession. Their experience reflects the broad Christian tradition.

The Twelve Steps

Step One: We admitted we were powerless over alcohol—that our lives had become unmanageable.

Step Two: Came to believe that a Power greater than ourselves could restore us to sanity.

Step Three: Made a decision to turn our will and our lives over to the care of God *as we understood him.*

Step Four: Made a searching and fearless moral inventory of ourselves.

Step Five: Admitted to God, to ourselves, and to another human being the exact nature of our wrongs.

Step Six: Were entirely ready to have God remove all these defects of character.

Step Seven: Humbly asked him to remove our shortcomings.

Step Eight: Made a list of all persons we had harmed, and
               became willing to make amends to them all.

Step Nine: Made direct amends to such people wherever
               possible, except when to do so would injure them
               or others.

Step Ten: Continued to take personal inventory and when
               we were wrong promptly admitted it.

Step Eleven: Sought through prayer and meditation to improve
               our conscious contact with God *as we understood
               Him*, praying only for knowledge of His will for us
               and the power to carry that out.

Step Twelve: Having had a spiritual awakening as the result of
               these steps, we tried to carry this message to
               alcoholics, and to practice these principles in all
               our affairs.

Self-searching ideally becomes a regular habit in the supportive community of an Alcoholics Anonymous group.

Confession to God needs to include our participation in corporate sins, such as institutional racism and pollution of the environment, as well as our unique, individual experience. The television news, the newspaper, a news magazine may stimulate awareness of the sins of our society in which we share responsibility. As the song "Carefully Taught" from the musical *South Pacific* points out, we learn from the time we are very young "to hate all the people [our] relatives hate." As we carry these hatreds unexamined into maturity, we share in the social sin of prejudice. As we practice the wasteful and self-indulgent lifestyle of an affluent society, we share in the deprivation and damage it causes.

Confession does not need to be a matter of wallowing in guilt or of self-flagellation. Confession can be thought of as a way of getting in touch with the growing edges of our Christian pilgrimage. It is a matter of acknowledging our reality to God who already knows and accepts us. Once we have confessed and repented, we can leave what has been to God, who then synthesizes and preserves what can be saved, and offers us new possibilities appropriate to where we are.

The more difficult part may be forgiving ourselves. When guilt continues to burden the spirit, some other problem may be involved. Guilt that is not relieved by confession and repentance may be neurotic guilt. Counseling or therapy may be necessary to get at its roots and to facilitate its release. Confessing to another person who can be trusted may help to sort out the problem. The Alcholics Anonymous system of sponsors and the Roman Catholic sacrament of confession testify to the value of working through guilt in dialogue with another person.

God's healing, whole-making, saving power can be at work in us in our prayers of confession and repentance. Like Isaiah, we can be set free to redirect our energies in more constructive directions. The author of James tells us: "Therefore confess your sins to one another, and pray for one another, that you may be healed" (James 5:16).

As we praise God and confess to God in prayer, we are turning toward reality—the reality that heals. In praise we open ourselves to God's reality, in confession to our own reality. In the familiar words of Henry Van Dyke:

> Joyful, joyful, we adore thee,
> God of glory, Lord of love;
> Hearts unfold like flowers before thee,
> Opening to the sun above.
> Melt the clouds of sin and sadness;
> Drive the dark of doubt away;
> Giver of immortal gladness,
> Fill us with the light of day!

Meditative Reading of Scripture

Having acknowledged God's presence and made confession to God, we are now ready to listen for God's word to us. Meditative reading of scripture is a primary resource for this dimension of prayer. The Bible records encounters between people and God over a period of nearly fifteen hundred years. God is revealed to us through the reports of the men and women whose stories are preserved for us there. God's nature and intentions are most clearly revealed to us in Jesus Christ. Meditating on scripture is an important part of being open *to* God.

Meditating on scripture, however, is different from looking at a work of art where the artist says that it can mean whatever you want it to mean. What is said in the Bible has come from a variety of sources, spoken, written, or sung in a variety of literary forms for a variety of purposes. The contents of the Bible have been used and shaped over the centuries by a community of faith for worship and instruction.

Scholars in recent years have pointed to the value of understanding the setting and the literary form and the function of a particular passage in order to get at its original meaning. Much new light has been thrown on scripture by this scholarly analysis, and some exciting discoveries have been made. One negative effect of this critical approach to scripture, however, is that it may prevent people who are not scholars from coming directly to the Bible for their own personal devotional life. The Bible, however, does not need to be given over to the private custody of the scholars. The Christian in the pew does not need to be limited to reading scripture through lenses provided by Bible scholars.

Many of the passages, themes, and forms that had one meaning when used originally in scripture reappear later with a new meaning and application. The New Testament includes an abundance of quotes and references from the Old Testament. Frequently an entirely new meaning is given to the old words. We do not need to be strictly limited to the original, historical meaning of passages of scripture in our understanding and interpretation of them. The original message is not the only message that it is legitimate for us to hear.

However, Christians do need to be alert to the danger of misusing scriptural materials. Literalism that ignores both cultural context and literary form and canonical themes can produce misinterpretations that violate the central truths of the Bible. Individual passages can be read to say what we want them to say.

James Sanders suggests that each passage should be read in light of some overall biblical agreements about God. In an article in *Horizons in Biblical Theology,* he suggests that "God is creator, elector, sustainer, judge, redeemer, and re-creator. And no passage should be read, or applied by the present reader without that affirmation clearly in mind."

No complete and final set of guidelines for devotional use of scripture, guaranteed to protect the reader from all error, has yet been developed. While we wait for such help, the Holy Spirit continues to speak to us directly through scripture. We can test our interpretations against the traditions of the Christian community, our reason, and our personal experience. We also have the gifts of interpretation provided by modern scholarship, a great deal of which is easily accessible to lay people.

Another rich resource for meditation is the wide range of translations of the Bible available to us today. The King James version continues to be published for those who respond to the poetic beauty of the language. A variety of translations into today's English can provide fresh insights by saying the same things with different words. Having more than one translation on hand can be stimulating to the imagination in the process of meditation or listening to God through scripture.

In meditating about God with scripture, two questions may be helpful. "What does this passage tell me about God?" "What does this tell me about the possibilities toward which God is calling all of the creation, including me?" Such thinking about God and listening for God's word can lead naturally to prayer or communion with God.

Petition

Another way we can pray is to tell God what we want and need. In the popular mind, that is a complete and adequate definition of prayer. In fact, prayer is sometimes regarded as nothing more than a twentiety-century form of primitive magic. In a television interview, a coach is asked what he plans to do to prepare for a game in which the odds are against him three to one. He answers, "Pray a lot!" A cartoon features two fish in a fishbowl over which is crouched a menacing cat. Eyeing a nearby telephone, one fish suggests, "Let's try Dial-a-Prayer!" On the golf course, a minister makes a "hole in one." His golfing partner challenges, "Don't tell me you haven't been praying!"

The desire to manipulate divine powers to human ends is characteristic of the most primitive of human religions. Much early religious ritual was an attempt to control the powers beyond human understanding to serve human purposes. Vestiges of this attitude are still with us.

Christian petition differs from magic in one major way. In Christian prayer, the goal is to communicate with God rather than to manipulate God. The individual's will is asserted and expressed in order that it can be harmonized with God's vision and purpose. In Christian prayer we tell God what we think we want and need. But these petitions are set in the context of a commitment to God. Jesus prayed, "Thy will be done" before he prayed "Give us this day our daily bread" (Matt. 6:10–11). In Gethsemane, he qualified his agonized plea "Let this cup pass from me" (Matt. 26:39) with "thy will be done" (Matt. 26:42).

P. T. Forsyth warns against the danger of letting our prayer be simply a total passivity before the will of God. Accepting a situation too quickly as God's will may be more a sign of weakness or immaturity than of faith and trust. Prayer is a matter of encounter of wills. Assertiveness is not a brand new value. In the parable of the woman who besieged an unjust judge, Jesus urged insistence in prayer. In Luke's words, "He told them a parable to the effect that they ought always to pray and not lose heart" (Luke 18:1–8). The Syrophoenician woman, by her assertiveness, convinced Jesus to change his mind and grant her request to free her daughter from a demon (Mark 7:25–30). To the woman with the issue of blood who touched his robe from behind in order to be healed, Jesus said, "Daughter, your faith has made you well; go in peace" (Luke 8:43–48). If we do not assert our will, it may be that God will not be able to offer us possibilities that would be available to us if we expressed our strength and will.

Forsyth also warns against being too timid in our prayers, too cautious in what we consider permissible subjects for petition. In his book *The Soul of Prayer,* Forsyth says, "Take everything to [God] that exercises you." Speaking of the intimate nature of our communion with God, he continues, "Faith means confidence between you [and God], and not only favours. And there is not confidence if you keep back what is hot or heavy on your heart.

Our Old Testament ancestors often had strong negative feelings, doubts, fears, grief, frustration, resentment, even anger toward God. There is no reason why this cannot be true for us. Being open *with* God in prayer will include dealing honestly with the issues of our lives, the things we are working on at the growing edges of our lives. All of that may not be pleasant to hear. But what close relationship is all sweetness and light?

Georgia Harkness joins P. T. Forsyth in encouraging boldness in prayer. In *Prayer and the Common Life,* she says, "Where there is any deep-seated need, it is fitting that such need be expressed before God in prayer." There is no need to limit the categories for our petitions. Many of the great prayers of the Christian church deal with requests for spiritual blessings, such as this prayer from "The Sacrament of the Lord's Supper or Holy Communion" from *The Book of Hymns.*

> Almighty God, unto whom all hearts are open, all desires known, and from whom no secrets are hid: Cleanse the thoughts of our hearts by the inspiration of thy Holy Spirit, that we may perfectly love thee, and worthily magnify thy holy name; through Christ our Lord. Amen.

But needs in all dimensions of our lives are objects of God's concern. We can pray for what we need physically, mentally, socially, and spiritually. If we are uncertain about the limits beyond which God does not go, Georgia Harkness counsels that, "The best course is to pray in humble trust and leave with God the boundaries of possibility."

She does add one pertinent word of warning to her encouragement to be bold in prayer. Prayer is misused when we think of it as a way to evade responsibility. According to Dr. Harkness, "It is not legitimate to pray for food, clothing, shelter, money for an education or a home, success in one's vocation, or any other material pursuit, and do nothing further about it." In general, however timidity and caution are the enemies of prayer.

We can expect that our petitions will be changed in the process of prayer about them. Our wishes and desires may well be clarified, purified, and matured. In the process of making our needs known to God, it may be helpful to ask, "Is there a deeper need behind my request? What is it that I *really* want?" The prayer itself may change several times in the process of being prayed before it can be answered in the context of God's broader vision. The starting place is "confidences," expecting purification in the process of praying rather than trying to do the screening before beginning to pray.

When we pray, we can trust the answers to God. God hears and takes account of our prayers. The answer may not be exactly what we asked, but God can be trusted to answer. And the answer can be expected to be consistent with God's overall creative and redemptive purposes.

Creative visualization is an increasingly popular way to pray for one's own needs. Instead of simply rehashing the problem or lamenting the situation, visualizing the ideal solution or the desired outcome can clarify the real need. Such positive imaging can sometimes help the one who prays to see ways to be the answer to one's own prayers. Psycho-cybernetics points to the power of such positive thinking in mobilizing the forces of our personality in our own interest. But positive visualization in prayer is more than autosuggestion. It is a way of clearly communicating with God what it is that we need.

Intercession

Creative visualization can also be helpful as a way to pray for others. Praying for others is one of the ways we can love our neighbors as ourselves. We can express love by giving to other people, by respecting their human dignity, by protesting and resisting those things that are destructive to human welfare, by ministering to human needs and working for better social conditions, by simple thoughtfulness and consideration. We can also love our neighbors by praying for them.

Prayer for each other is made possible by faith that we are all interconnected with each other in our mutual relationship with a God whose nature is love. It seems that physicists and philosophers and mystics are all talking about the organismic unity of reality. Twentieth-century physics has revealed to us a physical reality of interconnectedness in the universe. No person or thing is an island of independence. The distant moon affects the tides. A tiny virus triggers an international epidemic. One overloaded electric transformer throws a whole section of a nation into darkness. Every particle of energy is a part of a field of force that is in turn related to larger and larger fields of force throughout the universe. Everything each of us does affects the rest of reality. Every part of reality is related to every other part of reality in the universe. In the *Collected Papers of Evelyn Underhill,* the author relates this to prayer:

> The whole possibility of intercessory prayer seems based on this truth of spiritual communion—the fact that we are *not* separate little units but deeply interconnected—so that all we do, feel and endure has a secret effect, radiating far beyond ourselves.

From a philosopher's point of view, Alfred North Whitehead shows in *Process and Reality* that there is no philosophical reason why there cannot be a psychic field of force in reality along with the electromagnetic fields of force which science has so effectively identified and learned to use. He believes there may well be channels of communication through which our active benevolence shared with God in prayer can also directly contribute to the well-being of those for whom we pray.

God is related to all of the interconnected parts of the creation. God is the binding element in the world (See Session Two). God's relationship to all of this creation is expressed as creative-responsive love—active benevolence that will go to any length to do good to the beloved object and to secure its well-being—a relationship of devotion, loyalty, intimate knowledge, and responsibility.

God's love, which makes prayer for ourselves possible, is equally given to the people we love. God's love is given to the people who are like us and to the people who are different from us. It is given to those who are unattractive to us and to those who threaten us, to our enemies. God's care extends to the sparrows and the lilies of the field, to the trees and the stones, to the atoms and to the quarks and to the photons. Our neighbor can be understood to be the whole of creation. We are interconnected in God's love with all of the rest of reality.

When we pray for others, we join our psychic energy, our hearts, to the love of God in active benevolence. How this "works" remains a mystery. Archbishop William Temple, has been quoted as saying, "When I pray, coincidences happen; when I don't, they don't!"

At the least, in our prayers of intercession for others, we open ourselves to God's love for them. In so doing, we create the possibility of change in our attitudes toward them, and we make ourselves available as the instruments of God's love in their lives. In addition, we contribute our resources to the supply of love and caring in the world.

Praying for someone else can give direction to our efforts on their behalf. As we share our concern for them, we may receive new insight into what we can do. Our sensitivity may be enhanced and our motivation strengthened. Sometimes intercessory praying is all that we can do. We can pray with faith that, in cooperation with God's creative and healing love, forces are being released in ways that are beyond our understanding.

Intercession is not just to be for those for whom we feel natural love. "Love your enemies," said Jesus, "do good to those who hate you, bless those who curse you, pray for those who abuse you" (Luke 6:27–28). He demonstrated this love as he prayed from the cross, "Father, forgive them; for they know not what they do" (Luke 23:34). By praying for persons to whom we are not attracted or by whom we are threatened, we are drawn beyond our limited self-concern. We can see them against the background of their relationship with God. We can join with God in willing for them good things. Such intercession in the spirit of Christ has the power of creative transformation.

God receives and uses the good wishes for others that we offer in prayer, both in responding to us and in responding to those for whom we pray. God hears us when we bring the needs of others in our prayers. Alfred North Whitehead shares this insight in *Process and Reality:* "What is done in the world is transformed into a reality in heaven, and the reality in heaven passes back into the world. By reason of this reciprocal relation, the love in the world passes into the love in heaven, and floods back again into the world."

Most of what has been said so far has assumed the simplest type of intercession, one person praying for another. But intercession for people in groups, organizations, institutions, problem situations are all appropriate objects for our intercession. The liturgical prayers of the church have traditionally included prayers for the sick, the poor, the troubled, the lonely, victims of war, and other categories of people in special circumstances of need.

Such intercession involves positive thinking. Intercessory prayers that consist of thinking about all of the problems and pains and negative dimensions of a situation contribute nothing positive to either God or the world. Careful attention to what the other is experiencing, empathy with the other's pain, is an important part of preparation for intercession. Intercession itself involves sharing in the loving will of God. Visualization of our best wishes is one way to do this. Another way is to express hopes and wishes in words.

As we pray for the poor, we may find that God is leading us to envision and hope for an economic order in which all human beings will have access to the necessities of life. As we pray for victims of war, we may find ourselves led to envision peace and human community where justice is guaranteed for all. Prayers of intercession lead us to the petition "Thy kingdom come, thy will be done" (Matt. 6:10). And this prayer, of course, may be answered as we discover that we can make a contribution to alleviating some of the suffering about which we have shared our concern with God.

If we are willing to be led by the Spirit into interceding not only for those for whom we have natural concern, but to share in God's concern for all of the suffering of the world, our prayers will more nearly reflect the spirit of the Lord's Prayer.

Thanksgiving

It is appropriate to thank the Giver for the gifts. Praise and thanksgiving are sometimes difficult to distinguish from each other. Praise is our response to the being and presence of God, while thanksgiving is our response to God's gifts. But it is

76

possible to praise God for goodness and love revealed in gifts, while thanking God for the gift of divine presence.

Biblical prayers of thanksgiving mention the gifts of creation, provisions for our human needs, and God's saving work in our midst, especially God's love (1 Chron. 16:7–36; Psalms 30; 106).

Jesus gave thanks as he broke the bread and shared the cup with his disciples. Paul gave thanks to God for "the victory through our Lord Jesus Christ" (1 Cor. 15:57) and for God's "inexpressible gift" (2 Cor. 9:15). He also repeatedly gave thanks to God for the gift of his sisters and brothers in the faith. Thanksgiving to God is properly a part of both solitary and community worship. Martin Rinkart's well-known hymn is a prayer of thanksgiving:

> Now thank we all our God
> With heart and hands and voices,
> Who wondrous things hath done,
> In whom his world rejoices;
> Who, from our mothers' arms,
> Hath blessed us on our way
> With countless gifts of love,
> And still is ours today.

Such praying leads to still another way we can pray—the prayer of dedication.

Dedication

A prayer of dedication says to God, "We give this to be used for your purposes." A gesture of surrender of personal owner-ship is implied. Often such prayers begin by expressing awareness that everything is already God's, as in William W. How's hymn:

> We give thee but thine own,
> Whate'er the gift may be:
> All that we have is thine alone,
> A trust, O Lord, from thee.

A prayer of dedication is a normal part of our corporate worship. We make a dedication of our lives with the offerings at the altar. This is in the tradition of King David (1 Chron. 29:10–19). Special services of worship mark the dedication of new churches, schools, and homes. Solomon set the pattern with a lengthy prayer of dedication of the Temple of Jerusalem (1 Kings 8:23–53). Other prayers are expressions of personal dedication of self. One of the most poignant of these is a prayer written by Dietrich Bonhoeffer while he was a prisoner of the Nazis in Germany. It is included in *Letters and Papers from Prison:*

> Who am I? They often tell me
> I would step from my cell's confinement
> calmly, cheerfully, firmly,
> like a squire from his country-house.
>
> Who am I? They often tell me
> I would talk to my warders
> freely and friendly and clearly,
> as though it were mine to command.
>
> Who am I? They also tell me
> I would bear the days of misfortune
> equably, smilingly, proudly,
> like one accustomed to win.
>
> Am I then really all that which other men tell of?
> Or am I only what I myself know of myself,
> restless and longing and sick, like a bird in a cage,
> struggling for breath, as though hands were
> compressing my throat,
> yearning for colours, for flowers, for the voices of birds,
> thirsting for words of kindness, for neighborliness,
> trembling with anger at despotisms and petty humiliation,
> tossing in expectation of great events,
> powerlessly trembling for friends at an infinite distance,
> weary and empty at praying, at thinking, at making,
> faint, and ready to say farewell to it all?
>
> Who am I? This or the other?
> Am I one person today and tomorrow another?
> Am I both at once? A hypocrite before others,
> And before myself a contemptibly woebegone weakling?
> Or is something within me still like a beaten army,
> fleeing in disorder from victory already achieved?
>
> Who am I? They mock me, these lonely questions of mine.
> Whoever I am, thou knowest, O God, I am thine.

Contemplation

We can pray without words, in stillness or in contemplation. A contemplative monk, Thomas Merton, defined contemplative prayer as "a way of resting in [God] . . . it is a wordless and total surrender of the heart in silence" (*Contemplative Prayer*).

No method or system leads one into contemplative prayer. Sheer silence is not the same thing. As in a human relationship, the quiet, joyful resting in the presence of a loved one comes as a gift only after the work of getting acquainted and establishing ties of intimacy. According to Merton, the contemplative prayer of monks is "embedded in a life of psalmody, liturgical celebration and the meditative reading of Scripture." Such quiet resting is dependent on more active communion in an ongoing pattern.

In contemplative prayer there is a quiet communion of the self with God. Merton speaks of "silent and receptive attention to the inner working of the Holy Spirit." The unity of all things in God transcends the personal sense of self. Words and thoughts are no longer necessary, as one simply rests in God.

Mystical experiences of cosmic unity are fairly common for people who do not practice contemplative prayer. And it is possible for even one who is just beginning to pray to sit quietly in the presence of God. But those who feel called to the serious practice of contemplative prayer are encouraged to find a spiritual director, someone who has experience and who can be trusted to provide guidance along the way.

One of the profound insights provided by contemplative prayer is an intuitive awareness of the presence of God in all things. From the practice of such prayer in silence, it is possible to return to the kitchen, the classroom, the office and be aware of God in the glasses we wipe, the children we discipline, the job assigned to us, the people we meet. No longer is the world a lifeless machine. It is revealed as an ongoing process alive with the presence of God.

From the Eastern Orthodox branch of the Christian church has come a one-sentence prayer called the Jesus prayer which is used as a kind of mantra in contemplative prayer. The long form is "Lord Jesus Christ, Son of God, have mercy on me, a sinner." A short form, "Lord Jesus Christ, have mercy on me," is also frequently used. Sometimes the prayer is condensed into just the name "Jesus."

This prayer has been used in the eastern church since at least the sixth century. A collection of writings about the experience of people with the prayer is a part of the devotional tradition of that church. Only since the middle of the twentieth century has the prayer become popular in western Christendom.

One reason for the popularity of the Jesus prayer is that it capsulizes in just a few words the heart of Christian prayer. This means that it is ideal for busy people on the go. There is no need to settle down and get quiet. It can be prayed in the midst of activity. It can even be prayed in the heart in the middle of a conversation as a way of practicing the presence of God. The phrases of the prayer are often related to the rhythm of breathing. As a mantra, it can serve to center the self in the presence of God.

With or without a mantra, the thrust of Christian contemplative prayer is the constant awareness of the abiding presence of God. In Richard of Chichester's familiar words:

> Day by day,
> Dear Lord, of thee three things I pray:
> To see thee more clearly,
> Love thee more dearly,
> Follow thee more nearly,
> Day by day.

Conclusion

Material for this session has provided a brief, introductory overview of the major forms that Christian prayer has taken across the centuries. A public worship service may include all of the forms described or just a few. They may be in the order in which they are presented here or in some other order.

In personal devotion, the same is true. There is no set order in which one must pray. Prayer one day may be an overflowing of thanksgiving, another day fervent petition, and still another, quiet contemplation. Or a single prayer may include all of the forms. A period of meditative reading of scripture may lead one directly to intercessory prayer for some person or situation. While interceding one may be reminded of a neglected opportunity to do something for the person or about the situation, which may lead to confession. The confession may lead to a commitment to do something to make amends. Some other order of prayer may suggest itself. However, familiarity with the forms that prayer has taken in our tradition can enable us to progress in our prayers as the Spirit leads us.

A discussion of the question "How can we pray?" needs to include some words of warning.

1. Prayer takes time. Like any relationship, if our openness in

communion with God is to develop to any significant level, we will need to participate regularly in corporate worship, set aside regular time for individual prayer, and, if possible, spend some extended periods of time in meditation and prayer. Those who do this report that the benefits of such retreats convince them to make it a regular pattern.

2. There will be dry and frustrating times in prayer. All of the saints of the church who write about prayer report periods of discouragement and "dryness" in prayer. If this happens to you, don't give up. Sharing your pilgrimage in prayer with someone else or a group may help to sustain you through such times.

3. None of us ever becomes an "expert" in prayer. Even Thomas Merton, whose life was dedicated to prayer, wrote near the end of his life: "We do not want to be beginners. But let us be convinced of the fact that we will never be anything else but beginners, all our life!" (*Contemplative Prayer*)

QUESTIONS FOR REFLECTION AND DISCUSSION

1. With which of the ways we can pray do you have the most experience? Rank them in order of their familiarity to you. By number 1, write the way of praying with which you are most familiar, and so on. Select from: adoration, confession, meditative reading of scripture, petition, intercession, thanksgiving, dedication, and contemplation.

   1.
   2.
   3.
   4.
   5.
   6.
   7.
   8.

   Put a star after the ones you are willing to include in your private prayers this coming week.

2. Which of the ways we can pray is the most difficult for you?

81

Why is it difficult? Which is the easiest? Why is it easy?
3. Do you agree with the statement, "Every part of reality is related to every other part of reality in the universe"? How does your position on this issue affect the way you pray and think about prayer?
4. Have you observed any examples of prayer being used as modern magic? How was that different from prayer as petition?

A GUIDE FOR DAILY PRAYER: FOUR

Preparation and Centering

Worship God in the beauty of holiness; serve God with gladness, all the earth.
—Psalm 96:9 (AP)

Send your light and your truth, O God; may they lead me to you.
—Adapted from Psalm 43:3 (TEV)

Praise and Adoration

I will praise you, O God, with all my heart;
I will tell of all the wonderful things you have done.
I will sing with joy because of you.
I will sing praises to you,
You are fair and honest in your judgments,
You rule the world with righteousness,
You judge the nations with justice,
You are a refuge for the oppressed, a place of safety
in times of trouble,
Those who know you will trust you,
You do not abandon anyone who comes to you.
I will praise you, O God, with all my heart.
—Adapted from Psalm 9 (TEV)

Confession

Be merciful to me, O God,
because of your constant love.
I have sinned against you...
and done what you consider evil.

83

So you are right in judging me.
Remove my sin, and I will be clean. . . .
Create a pure heart in me, O God,
and put a new and loyal spirit in me.
    —Psalm 51:1, 4, 7, 10 (TEV)

Meditative Reading of Scripture

Day One—1 Corinthians 13:1–13
Day Two—Luke 8: 40–48
Day Three—John 15:1–11
Day Four—Isaiah 55:1–11
Day Five—Colossians 1:9–14
Day Six—Colossians 2:6–7, 18–19
Day Seven—Romans 11:33–36

Insights from the scriptures:

Petitions

Teach me to love as you have loved me, especially in this situation where it is hard for me to love. . . .

Plant your word in my heart. Nourish it and make it grow and bear fruit in my life. Prune from me all that is not fruitful.

I pray for healing of my body, my mind, and my spirit. Help me to do my part in releasing the springs of health that you have placed in me.

Fill me with the knowledge of your will and with all the wisdom and understanding that your Spirit gives as I confront the problems and decisions of this day.

I pray for. . . .

Intercessions

I pray for the oppressed of the world. Break the shackles that bind them. In their freedom, protect them from the temptation to become oppressors in their turn. . . .

I pray for those whose needs are in the news today. . . .

I pray for those whose needs are known only to themselves, the lonely, the proud, the isolated. Help me to reach out hands of compassion. Give me strength to help bear my sisters' and brothers' burdens; especially the burden carried by. . . .

I pray for those who have asked me to pray for them. . . .

I commit these prayers to you, trusting that your answers will be better than my asking.

Thanksgiving

O God, I see you before me at all times. You are near and I will not be troubled. So I am filled with gladness, and my words are full of joy. And I, mortal though I am, will rest assured in hope. You have shown me the paths that lead to life, and your presence fills me with joy. For these and all of your good gifts, I am thankful.
—Adapted from Acts 2:25–26, 28 (TEV)

Dedication

Whoever I am, you know, O God, I am yours!
—Adapted from "Who Am I?" by Dietrich Bonhoeffer

Silence

Benediction

God's peace, which is far beyond human understanding, will keep your heart and mind safe in union with Christ Jesus.
—Philippians 4:7 (AP)

SESSION FIVE: *What Difference Does Prayer Make?*

The television camera focused on Mother Teresa of Calcutta. Seated in a private jet, she was writing a letter. The narrator described how she handles the business of her worldwide religious order of a hundred thousand members with handwritten correspondence delivered by regular mail. She was hitching a ride out to look at some of her work in another Indian city. A bemused male voice from another part of the plane asked, "Where do you get all of your energy, Mother?" She lifted her head. Her tranquil, wrinkled face was framed by her blue and white habit. "That's why we go to the mass—communion," she said. "We start the day with Him and we end the day with Him." Members of her order work with the lepers, the indigent dying, the orphans, the poor of India. Those who live in the mother house in Calcutta are expected to be back from their day's work in time to be present at the evening worship. "We're not social workers, you know," she explains. Christian worship makes the difference.

Prayer Makes a Difference to the One Who Prays

Prayer is one means of grace—one of the ways in which God's healing, saving, whole-making work is done in the world. Prayer is given to us as a gift from God. When we appropriate this gift for ourselves, it can make a difference in us.

87

Martin Heidegger, the existentialist philosopher, has described two modes of being-in-the-world. In *Process Theology: An Introductory Exposition*, John Cobb and David Griffin quote Heidegger as saying that "One is the inauthentic mode in which one's projects are set for one by others—by social expectations or past conditioning or the hope of reward. The second is the authentic mode in which one chooses one's own projects." What has been said about prayer in this study suggests a third mode of being in which one chooses to create one's own life in dialogue with God.

Social pressures push and pull us in all sorts of directions. We are motivated to keep up with the Joneses, be accepted by the ingroup, be loved by desirable people. What we do can be powerfully influenced by what the Joneses, the ingroup, desirable people do, or by what we are told they expect. Much of commercial advertising hooks into our sensitivity to social expectations.

Past conditioning can set unrealistic limits on us, establish us in destructive behavior patterns, and predispose us to make faulty assumptions. The reward system of our society can entice us into doing things that violate both ourselves and our environment.

Other-directedness is to some degree desirable and unavoidable. Living cooperatively with other people involves negotiating our projects with the needs and expectations of others. Social expectations, conditioning, and reward systems make possible social existence. But life lived simply in unexamined response to the pressures exerted on us is not our only possibility. We do have the freedom to direct our lives from within. We can choose how to respond to all of the influences in our lives. We can establish our own value system and act out of it. We can choose how much power to give to the various forces at work on us.

One of the influences on our lives is the presence and call of God. God is with us, exerting an influence on us whether we choose to pay attention or not. When we choose to respond to God's offer of open communication, we choose to give power or weight to that relationship. We make an intentional move to give attention to the ideal possibilities that God offers to us. Without relinquishing our free will, we can freely choose to be Christian disciples. We can choose to live authentically in dialogue with God. Such open communion with God can creatively transform our lives.

WHAT DIFFERENCE DOES PRAYER MAKE?

In his letter to the church at Corinth, Paul talks about three qualities of Christian life, or fruits of the spirit: faith and hope and love (1 Cor. 13:13). When we pray, we open the way for the Spirit to nurture in us all three of these qualities—faith, hope, and love.

In a human friendship, communication and interaction are necessary if the relationship is to survive and grow. I need to know you in order to trust you. The only way we can get acquainted is by trusting each other enough to reveal ourselves. A little trust makes possible the first steps of friendship. This initial acquaintance makes possible more trust, which makes possible deeper friendship. So it is with prayer and faith. Faith expressed in prayer opens the way for the Spirit to nurture new faith, which in turn makes possible new adventures in prayer.

Thomas Merton points to this interdependence between prayer and faith in his remarks to a group of monks at a California monastery. According to Michael Terry, a member of that group, Merton advised them:

> Start where you are and deepen what you already have and you realize that you are already there. Everything has already been given to us in Christ. The trouble is that we don't know what we have. All we need is to experience what we already possess. The problem is that we don't slow down and take time to know it.

The Spirit also has an opportunity to nurture hope in us when we pray. Charles Wesley sang of his faith:

> Jesus, my strength, my hope,
> On thee I cast my care,
> With humble confidence look up,
> And know thou hearest my prayer.
> Give me on thee to wait,
> Till I can all things do,
> On thee, almighty to create,
> Almighty to renew.

In a discussion of worship in *Wrestle of Religion with Truth*, Henry Nelson Wieman remembers a street car that operated in Los Angeles in the early part of this century. At one point along its route it climbed a hill.

The hill is so steep that the car cannot use a trolley. It is lifted by a steel cable which runs endlessly beneath the car and between the rails. But the car does not move until it connects with the cable in proper manner. The car stands still until its passengers are in, then a certain clamping mechanism closes down upon the cable and the car is lifted to the top of the hill.

Worship, he says, is the way we clamp down on the cable. When we pray we discover that we are not alone. We are in God, and God is in us. We do not have to climb our hills in our own strength alone. We can tap into God's resources for our life. The resources of prayer are a source of hope.

In his sermon at Pentecost, Peter quotes from the Psalms, referring to the hope given by an awareness of God's presence.

> I saw the Lord always before me, for he is at my right hand that I may not be shaken; therefore my heart was glad, and my tongue rejoiced; moreover my flesh will dwell in hope . . . Thou hast made known to me the ways of life; thou wilt make me full of gladness with thy presence.
> —Acts 2:25–26, 28

A person who approaches life hopefully is more likely to be open to the new possibilities offered by God than is a person who is burdened with discouragement, locked in the grip of fear, inhibited by doubts. Communion with the "almighty to create, almighty to renew" is a channel for the sustenance of hope, a source of strength and energy, a medium through which the Spirit can be preparing us to receive possibilities that we might not otherwise even perceive.

In *The Meaning of Prayer,* Harry Emerson Fosdick illustrates the hope-inducing power of prayer with the story of Jem Nicholls, a "typical result of Quintin Hogg's work for boys in London."

> When Jem was asked, after Mr. Hogg's death, how the fight for character was coming on, he said, "I have a bit of trouble in keeping straight, but I thank God all is well. You see, I carry a photo of 'Q.H.' with me always, and whenever I am tempted, I take it out and his look is a wonderful help, and by the grace of God I am able to overcome all.

In prayer we discover that we have more than the resources with which our past has equipped us for facing the hills we have to climb.

When we pray, we give the Holy Spirit a chance to nurture in us love. Three kinds of love are involved: a healthy kind of self-esteem or respect and appreciation for the unique persons we have been created to be, a corresponding esteem for our human brothers and sisters combined with a willingness to care for them, and a deepening love for and commitment to God.

Church members occasionally object to the inclusion of a prayer of confession in the order of worship for the congregation. "It makes people feel bad," they say. "Confessing our offenses and our negligence stirs up guilt feelings and contributes to low self-esteem. People come to church to feel better, not to feel worse."

Christian confession, however, is a means of grace. When we confess who we really are to the One who already knows us and loves us as we really are, we have a chance at self-esteem grounded in personal integrity. God's acceptance and forgiveness does not say that everything we have done and left undone is all right. It says that we can pick up from here and move on. Freed from the burden of guilt, we can live with our real, sinful selves, accepting ourselves because God accepts us and esteeming ourselves because if God prizes us, how can we do otherwise?

Marjorie Suchocki points to the unique contribution that Christian confession makes to the development of healthy self-esteem. Speaking at a meeting of the American Academy of Religion, she noted that:

> There is . . . a source of identity for us beyond ourselves. That is, our identities do not depend solely upon our retention of the threads we have woven; if we let go of one self-image, it is not the case that we will succumb to the chaos of fragmentation and fear. . . . We can dare to let it go, knowing there is a ground to the self we receive in its stead. The new self-image, constructed in openness to all of the past, will be congruent with reality. Therefore, the energies previously utilized in denial of reality will now be released for ways of transformation.

The forgiveness is offered. The prayer of confession opens the way for that forgiveness to be operative in our lives. Confession makes an important contribution to the development of healthy self-love.

Prayers of intercession make a contribution to the development of our love for others. Our ability to love other people grows with practice. We learn to love by giving love. In our prayers of intercession, we are expressing our care and concern

91

for other people to God who also loves and is concerned for them. If I pray for you, the Holy Spirit has an opportunity to be at work in me, increasing my love and concern for you. My prayer may be answered with a fresh insight about what I can do to contribute to your well-being. As I express my love for you, my love can grow. Prayers for people for whom we have little concern may give the Holy Spirit an opportunity to nurture love and concern for them in us. Prayers for our enemies give the Holy Spirit a chance to show us ways to deal constructively with the conflict or enmity between us. Acting on such insights opens the way for improved relationships and moves us in the direction of love.

At the least, prayers of intercession stretch us beyond self-centeredness and widen the horizons of our concern. As we open ourselves to God's love for other people, some of that compassion may rub off on us. Mother Teresa, for example, says that she sees Christ dying in the gutter in Calcutta. When we give God a chance, we may find ourselves sent out as agents of divine love. Norman Pittenger describes this process in *Praying Today*: "The Love that is God awakens, stimulates, and strengthens the capacity for loving that is God's very image in [humanity]."

When we pray, we give the Holy Spirit an opportunity to increase in us love for God. When we take time for adoration, praise, and thanksgiving, we open ourselves up to more profound comprehension of who God is and what God does. An expanded and clarified vision of God has enhanced power to evoke from us devotion. As we grow in prayer, our increased experience with God can lead to a deeper love for God. This, at least, is the witness of the saints of the church.

Other words besides faith and hope and love have been used to describe the work of the Holy Spirit in the one who communicates openly with God. Trust, confidence, power, strength, patience, peace, tranquility of soul, personal integration, an attitude of gratitude, even "recharged batteries" are identified as by-products of prayer. And there is abundant testimony that through the life of prayer the spirit of Christ can come into a human life. William James once said that we become like what we attend to.

When we open ourselves in prayer, we respond to the invitation offered in Revelation 3:20: "Behold, I stand at the door and knock; if any one hears my voice and opens the door, I will come in to him and eat with him, and he with me." In the words of John Cobb, writing in *Process Theology: An Introductory Exposition:*

"Christ is most fully present in human beings when they are most fully open to that presence."

Paul speaks about the Spirit dwelling in us: "If the Spirit of him who raised Jesus from the dead dwells in you, he who raised Christ Jesus from the dead will give life to your mortal bodies also through his Spirit which dwells in you" (Rom. 8:11). Sometimes it is Christ who dwells in us. "To them God chose to make known how great among the Gentiles are the riches of the glory of this mystery, which is Christ in you, the hope of glory" (Col. 1:27). And sometimes Paul speaks of growing up into Christ, or putting on Christ (Gal. 3:27). The gospel writer John, on the other hand, reports that Christ spoke of himself as the vine, his human disciples as the branches (John 15:5).

In multiple ways the message is communicated that God can live in and through us. As we practice being open to God, the divine likeness can grow in us. Our desires can be purified, a new value system can evolve, we can become new people. In *The Jesus Prayer,* Per-Olaf Sjogren reveals that:

> When [Christ] lives in my heart, then he also shines through; when praise of him is singing in my heart, then it also rings through, often without my knowing. It is not my personality but his that becomes luminous.

All that has been said to this point about the difference prayer can make to an individual can be said also about the church. As the church opens to God in prayer, it gives the Holy Spirit an opportunity to nurture its faith, its hope, its love, and to make it the body of Christ in the world.

But the experience of praying together has the additional power to bind a community of believers to each other. The shared relationship to God in worship provides the basis of unity for a shared mission in the world as God's people. The mission of the church has its roots in the worship of God in the church. From the prayers of the congregation come the power and direction for the work of the church in service in the world.

Prayer Makes a Difference to the World

Prayer makes a difference beyond the Christian and the church. It makes a difference to the world. The individual Christian in whom the Holy Spirit is at work makes a difference.

So it is a good thing that there are people in whose heart Christ dwells. Even one person who has in his heart not a den of thieves but a temple where Christ dwells is an immeasurable blessing for any home, or group, or community. That person carries a lighted candle, the beams of which shine on all whom he meets, on all with whom he has to do. It is not he who shines on the others about him; it is Christ shining in and through him.

   —*The Jesus Prayer* by Per-Olaf Sjogren

Beyond this, the prayer itself affects the world. Our prayers make a positive contribution to reality. There is considerable evidence that in the interconnectedness of all reality, our prayers for others and for the world make a difference to those for whom we pray.

Prayer Makes a Difference to God

And our prayers make a difference to God. When we pray, we make a way for God's grace to be active in our lives. We provide an opportunity for God's saving, healing, whole-making work in us. As we offer ourselves as God's instruments in the world, God can work not only in us but through us.

Our petitions and intercessions influence God's activity. We do not change God's vision of the ideal possibilities for the creation. But we can affect what God does in a particular concrete situation. God hears all of our prayers and takes them all into account. Our prayers are answered. Many are answered just as we ask them. Others are not. To some of the petitions, the answer may be "No." Other petitions need to be matured and purified in the dialogue of prayer before they can be answered in the context of God's active benevolence toward the whole creation.

How God answers prayer is sometimes beyond our thoughts, and God's ways are not our ways (Isa. 55:8–9). But there is an unending parade of witnesses to answered prayer. In response to prayer, circumstances change; problems untangle; tensions ease; a clear conviction emerges about an alternative accompanied by the kind of peace and joy that only God can give; a new idea or perspective lights up the mind; fresh courage, calm, comfort or hope emerges; a nudge to do something is felt; a new desire appears; a temptation diminishes or is conquered; a soul is strengthened; a door opens. God acts in response to what we ask.

And beyond this, some people make so bold as to suggest that

WHAT DIFFERENCE DOES PRAYER MAKE?

God is enriched by our sharing in prayer, that as we express adoration and thanksgiving and share ourselves in confession, petition, intercession, and dedication—as we rest in God's presence in contemplation—we even contribute to God's pleasure!

Is it any wonder that Christians have understood prayer to be a part of God's will for our lives?

QUESTIONS FOR REFLECTION AND DISCUSSION

1. What needs to be added to this statement about the difference prayer makes?
2. Does anything not ring true with your experience? Is there anything with which you disagree?
3. Has prayer ever been for you the clamping down on a cable that could carry you up a hill? What about prayer do you think caused Henry Nelson Wieman to think of that image?
4. How are the members of Mother Teresa's order different from social workers?

A GUIDE FOR DAILY PRAYER: FIVE

During the last week of this study, create your own order of prayer. Drawing on your own experience, scripture, and the liturgical resources of the church, create a prayer experience to share with your study group, or to use alone, that makes possible openness to God and with God for you.

Perhaps you can begin a more long-range program of reading the scripture. Two popular patterns merit your consideration.

1. Follow a daily lectionary. The lectionary at the end of this book suggests three scripture lessons for each day for a year beginning with the first Sunday in Advent. Over the year, major portions of scripture will be covered. The passages will relate to the seasons of the church year—Advent, Christmas, Easter, and Pentecost. Many ministers preach from a lectionary. This might be a way to link your personal devotional reading to the themes highlighted in the corporate worship of your congregation.

2. Choose one or two books from the Bible and read one or two chapters from each during the week. For example, you might begin with the Psalms and the Gospel according to John. Reading background on the book chosen before beginning to read it devotionally can help you understand the context of what you are reading. A wide variety of bible study resources can help you know what scholars have learned about the material you are reading. This may stimulate you to hear more than you might otherwise hear. Beware, however, of getting sidetracked into doing nothing but objective Bible study. Let the Spirit speak to you through the scriptures.

If you are going to continue to work with a prayer partner, or "soul friend" or group, you might agree to read the same passages and share your insights when you meet to share in prayer.

Suggestions for Group Leaders

This study can be used in many settings with many teaching-learning styles. Classes with a lecture-discussion format can use the material in the chapters as already presented. Prayer groups can incorporate the discussion questions and prayer guides with time for group prayer. Small groups can read together and share their responses to the questions.

Groups meeting for longer sessions or using the material in retreat settings may want to vary their activities using some of the following suggestions. These are not intended to be session plans, just ideas to be incorporated in whatever format the group chooses. They are suggested in relationship to specific chapters, but may fit in more than one area equally well.

Session One: Introduction to Prayer and Praying

1. Have someone lead the group in the process of centering, using the suggestions on pages 11 and 12. Remember to give a space of silence between suggestions so that people can do what has been suggested. Close the centering with prayer, and give the group members a minute to "come back to the group."

Session Two: How Can We Think About God?

1. Share from the experience with a personal devotional time

97

during the week. If members of your group are using the guides for daily prayer, you may want to begin each session by asking the following questions:

a. What have you learned about prayer from meditative reading of the suggested passages of scripture for this week (or session)?

b. What happened to you in your experience of prayer? How is it going? Retreat groups can use the scripture passages suggested in the daily prayer guides for small group study or group worship.

2. Fill out the chart on pages 40–42. Discuss the stars and the x's and the additions to the list.

3. Lead the group in a meditation.
Read Isaiah 54:10 aloud. Before a second reading say to the group: "Close your eyes and listen to this passage as a personal address to you." Read Isaiah 49:15–16. Before a second reading, say to the group: "Listen to this passage, putting your own name in the place of Jerusalem."

4. Use the chart on pages 40–42 as a basis for meditation. Say to the class: "Choose three statements about God that you affirm and that help you to pray. Phrase them so that they relate to you personally right now: God is with me; God loves me; God is affected by what I do. Reflect silently on these affirmations of faith and what they mean for your life."
Close these meditations with prayer.

Session Three: How Can We Think About Prayer?

1. Practice openness *with* God. Give each person a sheet of paper and a pencil and suggest that they write a letter to God describing exactly "What it is like to be you right now." Share with God joys and sorrows, pains and pleasures, thanksgivings and needs as honestly as possible. These letters can be kept as a part of a personal journal.

2. Practice openness *to* God. Read together a passage of scripture. Ask class members to identify with the person to whom the message is given. Ask them to reflect on how that message relates to their lives now. For example, read Luke 9:57–62. Have each person ask silently, "What excuses do I give when Jesus says to me, 'Follow me'? What do I need to let go of in order to be of use to the kingdom?" Listen openly to what God may be saying to you. In small groups, you may want to talk about this experience, sharing what happened to you,

what was easy, what was difficult. Sharing, of course, should be voluntary.

3. Lead the group in a breathing meditation.
"Close your eyes and concentrate on your breathing. Relax and center. When you have become quiet, say to yourself as you inhale, 'Thankfully, I breathe in God's love.' As you exhale, say to yourself, 'Joyfully, I pass it on to the world.'"

Session Four: How Can We Pray?

1. Write and share prayers of praise and adoration. Provide for each person a hymnal, a Bible, paper and pencil, and a list of praise psalms and praise hymns. After an introduction to prayer as praise and adoration, provide fifteen to twenty minutes for quiet reading from these treasuries of praise. Then allow ten minutes for each person to write a personal prayer of praise to God. If time permits, share these prayers in the group or in small groups of four to six.
Praise Psalms: 8, 19, 24, 33, 92, 98, 100, 103, 111, 150
Praise Hymns: *O for a Thousand Tongues to Sing*
Sing Praise to God Who Reigns Above
Stand Up and Bless the Lord
How Great Thou Art
Come, Let Us Tune Our Loftiest Song
Immortal, Invisible, God Only Wise
Praise to the Living God
For the Beauty of the Earth
I Sing the Almighty Power of God
Let All On Earth Their Voices Raise
O How Glorious, Full of Wonder
The Spacious Firmament on High
This Is My Father's World
Now Thank We All Our God
Praise to the Lord, the Almighty
All Creatures of Our God and King
Praise, My Soul, the King of Heaven

2. Invite someone from Alcoholics Anonymous to describe the meaning of confession in the A. A. experience.

3. Read aloud the biblical story of the woman with the issue of blood (Mark 5:25–34). Invite group members to identify with her in the story in silent meditation, using the senses to see, hear, smell, feel what she saw, heard, smelled, felt as she came to Jesus in her desperate search for healing. Ask them

to identify what needs they might bring to Jesus, what sources of pain, what needs for healing in their own lives. Close with a time of prayer when these needs can be shared with God, in silence or in shared petition.

4. Bring prayer lists for personal journals. Give group members time to list specific prayers for their own deepest needs and intercessions for others for their prayer lists.

5. Read over together the "Wesleyan Covenant Service" from the United Methodist *Book of Worship*, paying special attention to the prayer of dedication.

6. With the leader watching the clock, let the group spend fifteen minutes in silent meditation. Close this time with a brief, spoken prayer.

Session Five: What Difference Does Prayer Make?

1. Ask again: "What blocks you from growing in prayer?" and "What helps you grow in prayer?" Discuss together ways to remove blocks and strengthen those forces which help.

2. Look at possibilities for creative personal patterns for private devotion. Consider support systems such as prayer partners and prayer groups.

Bibliography

Books

Alcoholics Anonymous. *Twelve Steps and Twelve Traditions*. New York: Alcoholics Anonymous World Services, 1952.

Barth, Karl. *Prayer According to the Catechisms of the Reformation*. Philadelphia: Westminster Press, 1952.

Bauman, Edward. *Intercessory Prayer*. Philadelphia: Westminster Press, 1958.

Bloesch, Donald G. *The Struggle of Prayer*. New York: Harper, 1980.

Bloom, Anthony. *Beginning to Pray*. Paramus, N.J.: Paulist/Newman Press, 1970.

_____. *Living Prayer*. Springfield, Ill.: Templegate Publishers, 1975.

Bonhoeffer, Dietrich. *Prisoner for God*. Edited by Eberhard Bethge. New York: Macmillan, 1953.

Book of Hymns: Official Hymnal of the United Methodist Church. Nashville: United Methodist Publishing House, 1966.

Cargas, Harry James and Lee, Bernard, eds. *Religious Experience and Process Theology*. New York: Paulist/Newman Press, 1976.

The Cloud of Unknowing. By an English Mystic of the Fourteenth Century. Edited by James Walsh. New York: Paulist/Newman Press, 1981.

Cobb, John B., Jr. *A Christian Natural Theology*. Philadelphia: Westminster Press, 1965.

_____. *God and the World*. Philadelphia: Westminster Press, 1969.

_____. *To Pray or Not to Pray*. Nashville: Upper Room, 1974.

_____, and Griffin, David Ray. *Process Theology: An Introductory Exposition*. Philadelphia: Westminster Press, 1976.

De Caussade, Jean-Pierre. *Abandonment to the Divine Providence*. Garden City, N.Y.: Doubleday, 1975.

101

Dunnam, Maxie. *The Workbook of Intercessory Prayer.* Nashville: Upper Room, 1974.

──────. *The Workbook of Living Prayer.* Nashville: Upper Room, 1974.

Forsyth, Peter Taylor. *The Soul of Prayer.* London: Independent Press, 1916.

Fosdick, Harry Emerson. *The Meaning of Prayer.* Folcroft, Pa.: Folcroft Library Editions, 1976.

Fox, Matthew. *On Becoming a Musical Mystical Bear: Spirituality American Style.* New York: Paulist/Newman Press, 1976.

Gawain, Shakti. *Creative Visualization.* Berkeley, Calif.: Whatever Publishing, 1978.

Grou, Jean. *How to Pray.* Greenwood, S.C.: Attic Press, 1964.

Harkness, Georgia E. *Mysticism: Its Meaning and Message.* Nashville: Abingdon Press, 1973.

──────. *Prayer and the Common Life.* Nashville: Abingdon Press, 1948.

Heiler, Friedrich. *Prayer: A Study in the History and Psychology of Religion.* Translated and edited by Samuel McComb. London: Oxford University Press, 1932.

Hymnal of the Protestant Episcopal Church in the U.S.A. New York: Church Pension Fund, 1940.

Interpreter's Dictionary of the Bible. 5 Vols. Nashville: Abingdon Press, 1976.

Johnston, William. *Still Point: Reflections on Zen and Christian Mysticism.* Bronx: Fordham University Press, 1980.

Jones, Rufus. *Rufus Jones Speaks to Our Time: An Anthology.* Edited by Harry Emerson Fosdick. New York: Macmillan, 1951.

Kelly, Thomas. *A Testament of Devotion.* New York: Harper, 1941.

Kelsey, Morton T. *The Other Side of Silence.* New York: Paulist/Newman Press, 1976.

Leech, Kenneth. *True Prayer.* New York: Harper, 1981.

Lewis, C.S. *Letters to Malcolm: Chiefly on Prayer.* New York: Harcourt Brace Jovanovich, 1973.

Link, Mark. *Breakaway.* Allen, Tex.: Argus Communications, 1980.

Magee, John. *Reality and Prayer.* Nashville: Abingdon Press, 1978.

Maloney, George. *Inward Stillness.* Danville, N.J.: Dimension Books, 1976.

Merton, Thomas. *Contemplative Prayer.* Garden City, N.Y.: Doubleday, 1971.

Oliver, Fay Conlee. *Christian Growth Through Meditation.* Valley Forge, Pa.: Judson Press, 1976.

Pittenger, Norman. *God's Way with Men.* Valley Forge, Pa.: Judson Press, 1969.

──────. *Praying Today.* Grand Rapids: Eerdmans, 1974.

Schillebeeckx, Edward and Van Iersel, Bas, eds. *A Personal God.* New York: Crossroads Press, 1977.

Simpson, Robert L. *The Interpretation of Prayer in the Early Church.* Philadelphia: Westminster Press, 1965.

BIBLIOGRAPHY

Sjogren, Per-Olaf. *The Jesus Prayer.* Philadelphia: Fortress Press, 1975.

Stahl, Carolyn. *Opening to God.* Nashville: Upper Room, 1977.

Teresa of Avila, St. *The Way of Perfection.* Garden City, N.Y.: Doubleday, 1972.

Underhill, Evelyn. *Concerning the Inner Life.* New York: Dutton, 1926.

———. *Collected Papers of Evelyn Underhill.* Ed. by Lucy Menzies. London: Longmans Green, 1946.

Ware, Kallistos. *The Power of the Name: The Jesus Prayer in Orthodox Spirituality.* Fairacres, Oxford: SLG Press, 1974.

The Way of a Pilgrim. Translated from the Russian by R. M. French. New York: The Seabury Press, 1965.

Webb, Lance. *The Art of Personal Prayer.* Nashville: Upper Room, 1977.

Whitehead, Alfred North. *Adventures of Ideas.* New York: The Free Press, 1967.

———. *Process and Reality.* Corrected Edition. New York: The Free Press, 1978.

———. *Religion in the Making.* New York: New American Library, 1974.

———. *Science and the Modern World.* New York: The Free Press, 1967.

Wieman, Henry Nelson. *The Wrestle of Religion with Truth.* New York: Macmillan, 1928.

Wright, John H. *A Theology of Christian Prayer.* New York: Pueblo Publishing, 1979.

Articles

Gray, Donald P. "Prayer: Passing Over and Coming Back," *Worship* 48 (1974)

Saliers, Donald E. "Theology and Prayer: Some Conceptual Reminders," *Worship* 48 (1974)

Sanders, James A. "Canonical Context and Canonical Criticism," *Horizons in Biblical Theology: An International Dialogue* 2 (1980)

Daily Lectionary

This lectionary has been adapted from the "Daily Office Lectionary" in the *Book of Common Prayer*. The lectionary begins on the first Sunday of Advent. Three readings are provided for each Sunday and weekday. Two of the readings may be used in the morning and one in the evening; or, if the lectionary is read only once in the day, all three readings may be used. When more than one reading is used, the first is always from the Old Testament. Any reading may be lengthened at discretion. Suggested lengthenings are shown in parentheses.

In this lectionary (except in the weeks from 4 Advent to 1 Epiphany, and Palm Sunday to 2 Easter), the Psalms are arranged in a seven-week pattern which recurs throughout the year, except for appropriate variations during Lent and Easter. You will note that the readings from Psalms are listed first for each day and that these biblical citations do not include the word "Psalms."

In the citation of Psalms, those for the morning are given first, and then those for the evening. Any of the Psalms listed for a given day may be used in the morning or in the evening. Likewise, Psalms listed for any day may be used on any other day in the same week.

Brackets and parentheses are used (brackets in the case of whole Psalms, parentheses in the case of verses) to indicate Psalms and verses which may be omitted. In some instances, the entire portion of the psalter has been bracketed and alternative psalmody provided. Those who desire to recite the psalter in its entirety should, in each instance, use the bracketed Psalms rather than the alternatives.

Week of 1 Advent

Sunday	146, 147 ❋ 111, 112, 113	
	Isa. 1:1-9 2 Pet. 3:1-10 Matt. 25:1-13	
Monday	1, 2, 3 ❋ 4, 7	
	Isa. 1:10-20 1 Thess. 1:1-10 Luke 20:1-8	
Tuesday	5, 6 ❋ 10, 11	
	Isa. 1:21-31 1 Thess. 2:1-12 Luke 20:9-18	
Wednesday	119:1-24 ❋ 12, 13, 14	
	Isa. 2:1-11 1 Thess. 2:13-20 Luke 20:19-26	
Thursday	18:1-20 ❋ 18:21-50	
	Isa. 2:12-22 1 Thess. 3:1-13 Luke 20:27-40	
Friday	16, 17 ❋ 22	
	Isa. 3:8-15 1 Thess. 4:1-12 Luke 20:41—21:4	
Saturday	20, 21:1-7(8-14) ❋ 110:1-5(6-7), 116, 117	
	Isa. 4:2-6 1 Thess. 4:13-18 Luke 21:5-19	

Week of 2 Advent

Sunday	148, 149, 150 ❋ 114, 115
	Isa. 5:1-7 2 Pet. 3:11-18 Luke 7:28-35
Monday	25 ❋ 9, 15
	Isa. 5:8-12, 18-23 1 Thess. 5:1-11 Luke 21:20-28
Tuesday	26, 28 ❋ 36, 39
	Isa. 5:13-17, 24-25 1 Thess. 5:12-28 Luke 21:29-38
Wednesday	38 ❋ 119:25-48
	Isa. 6:1-13 2 Thess. 1:1-12 John 7:53—8:11
Thursday	37:1-18 ❋ 37:19-42
	Isa. 7:1-9 2 Thess. 2:1-12 Luke 22:1-13
Friday	31 ❋ 35
	Isa. 7:10-25 2 Thess. 2:13—3:5 Luke 22:14-30
Saturday	30, 32 ❋ 42, 43
	Isa. 8:1-15 2 Thess. 3:6-18 Luke 22:31-38

Week of 3 Advent

Sunday	63:1-8(9-11), 98 ❋ 103
	Isa. 13:6-13 Heb. 12:18-29 John 3:22-30
Monday	41, 52 ❋ 44
	Isa. 8:16—9:1 2 Pet. 1:1-11 Luke 22:39-53
Tuesday	45 ❋ 47, 48
	Isa. 9:1-7 2 Pet. 1:12-21 Luke 22:54-69
Wednesday	119:49-72 ❋ 49,[53]
	Isa. 9:8-17 2 Pet. 2:1-10a Mark 1:1-8
Thursday	50 ❋ [59, 60] or 33
	Isa. 9:18—10:4 2 Pet. 2:10b-16 Matt. 3:1-12
Friday	40, 54 ❋ 51
	Isa. 10:5-19 2 Pet. 2:17-22 Matt. 11:2-15
Saturday	55 ❋ 138, 139:1-17(18-23)
	Isa. 10:20-27 Jude 17-25 Luke 3:1-9

Week of 4 Advent

Sunday	24, 29 ❋ 8, 84
	Isa. 42:1-12 Eph. 6:10-20 John 3:16-21
Monday	61, 62 ❋ 112, 115
	Isa. 11:1-9 Rev. 20:1-10 John 5:30-47
Tuesday	66, 67 ❋ 116, 117
	Isa. 11:10-16 Rev. 20:11—21:8 Luke 1:5-25
Wednesday	72 ❋ 111, 113
	Isa. 28:9-22 Rev. 21:9-21 Luke 1:26-38
Thursday	80 ❋ 146, 147
	Isa. 29:13-24 Rev. 21:22—22:5 Luke 1:39-48a(48b-56)
Friday	93, 96 ❋ 148, 150
	Isa. 33:17-22 Rev. 22:6-11, 18-20 Luke 1:57-66
Dec. 24	45, 46 ❋ ——
	Isa. 35:1-10 Rev. 22:12-17, 21 Luke 1:67-80
Christmas Eve	—— ❋ 89:1-29
	Isa. 59:15b-21 Phil. 2:5-11

Christmas Day and Following

Christmas Day	2, 85 ❋ 110:1-5(6-7), 132
	Zech. 2:10-13 1 John 4:7-16 John 3:31-36
First Sunday after Christmas	93, 96 ❋ 34
	Isa. 62:6-7, 10-12 Heb. 2:10-18 Matt. 1:18-25
Dec. 29	18:1-20 ❋ 18:21-50*
	Isa. 12:1-6 Rev. 1:1-8 John 7:37-52
Dec. 30	20, 21:1-7(8-14) ❋ 23, 27
	Isa. 25:1-9 Rev. 1:9-20 John 7:53—8:11
Dec. 31	46, 48 ❋ ——
	Isa. 26:1-9 2 Cor. 5:16—6:2 John 8:12-19
New Year's Eve	—— ❋ 90
	Isa. 65:15b-25 Rev. 21:1-6
New Year's Day	103 ❋ 148
	Gen. 17:1-12a, 15-16 Col. 2:6-12 John 16:23b-30
Second Sunday after Christmas	66, 67 ❋ 145
	Col. 3:12-17 1 John 2:12-17 John 6:41-47
Jan. 2	34 ❋ 33
	Gen. 12:1-7 Heb. 11:1-12 John 6:35-42, 48-51
Jan. 3	68 ❋ 72**
	Gen. 28:10-22 Heb. 11:13-22 John 10:7-17
Jan. 4	85, 87 ❋ 89:1-29**
	Exod. 3:1-12 Heb. 11:23-31 John 14:6-14
Jan. 5	2, 110:1-5(6-7) ❋ ——
	Joshua 1:1-9 Heb. 11:32—12:2 John 15:1-16
Eve of Epiphany	—— ❋ 29, 98
	Isa. 66:18-23 Rom. 15:7-13

*If today is Saturday, use Psalms 23 and 27 at Evening Prayer.
**If today is Saturday, use Psalm 136 at Evening Prayer.

The Epiphany and Following

Epiphany	46, 97 ❋ 96, 100
	Isa. 52:7-10 Rev. 21:22-27 Matt. 12:14-21
*Jan. 7**	103 ❋ 114, 115
	Isa. 52:3-6 Rev. 2:1-7 John 2:1-11
Jan. 8	117, 118 ❋ 112, 113
	Isa 59:15-21 Rev. 2:8-17 John 4:46-54
Jan. 9	121, 122, 123 ❋ 131, 132
	Isa. 63:1-5 Rev. 2:18-29 John 5:1-15
Jan. 10	138, 139:1-17(18-23) ❋ 147
	Isa. 65:1-9 Rev. 3:1-6 John 6:1-14
Jan. 11	148, 150 ❋ 91, 92
	Isa. 65:13-16 Rev. 3:7-13 John 6:15-27
Jan. 12	98, 99, [100] ❋ ——
	Isa. 66:1-2, 22-23 Rev. 3:14-22 John 9:1-12, 35-38
Eve of 1 Epiphany	—— ❋ 104
	Isa. 61:1-9 Gal. 3:23-29; 4:4-7

Week of 1 Epiphany

Sunday	146, 147 ❋ 111, 112, 113
	Isa. 40:1-11 Heb. 1:1-12 John 1:1-7, 19-20, 29-34
Monday	1, 2, 3 ❋ 4, 7
	Isa. 40:12-23 Eph. 1:1-14 Mark 1:1-13
Tuesday	5, 6 ❋ 10, 11
	Isa. 40:25-31 Eph. 1:15-23 Mark 1:14-28
Wednesday	119:1-24 ❋ 12, 13, 14
	Isa. 41:1-16 Eph. 2:1-10 Mark 1:29-45
Thursday	18:1-20 ❋ 18:21-50
	Isa. 41:17-29 Eph. 2:11-22 Mark 2:1-12
Friday	16, 17 ❋ 22
	Isa. 42:(1-9)10-17 Eph. 3:1-13 Mark 2:13-22
Saturday	20, 21:1-7(8-14) ❋ 110:1-5(6-7), 116, 117
	Isa. 43:1-13 Eph. 3:14-21 Mark 2:23—3:6

*The Psalms and readings for the dated days after the Epiphany are used only until the following Saturday evening.

Week of 2 Epiphany

Sunday   148, 149, 150 ✣ 114, 115
Isa. 43:14—44:5   Heb. 6:17—7:10   John 4:27-42

Monday   25 ✣ 9,15
Isa. 44:6-8, 21-23   Eph. 4:1-16   Mark 3:7-19a

Tuesday   26, 28 ✣ 36, 39
Isa. 44:9-20   Eph. 4:17-32   Mark 3:19b-35

Wednesday   38 ✣ 119:25-48
Isa. 44:24—45:7   Eph. 5:1-14   Mark 4:1-20

Thursday   37:1-18 ✣ 37:19-42
Isa. 45:5-17   Eph. 5:15-33   Mark 4:21-34

Friday   31 ✣ 35
Isa. 45:18-25   Eph. 6:1-9   Mark 4:35-41

Saturday   30, 32 ✣ 42, 43
Isa. 46:1-13   Eph. 6:10-24   Mark 5:1-20

Week of 3 Epiphany

Sunday   63:1-8(9-11), 98 ✣ 103
Isa. 47:1-15   Heb. 10:19-31   John 5:2-18

Monday   41, 52 ✣ 44
Isa. 48:1-11   Gal. 1:1-17   Mark 5:21-43

Tuesday   45 ✣ 47, 48
Isa. 48:12-21   Gal. 1:18—2:10   Mark 6:1-13

Wednesday   119:49-72 ✣ 49,[53]
Isa. 49:1-12   Gal. 2:11-21   Mark 6:13-29

Thursday   50 ✣ [59, 60] or 118
Isa. 49:13-23   Gal. 3:1-14   Mark 6:30-46

Friday   40, 54 ✣ 51
Isa. 50:1-11   Gal. 3:15-22   Mark 6:47-56

Saturday   55 ✣ 138, 139:1-17(18-23)
Isa. 51:1-8   Gal. 3:23-29   Mark 7:1-23

Week of 4 Epiphany

Sunday   24, 29 ✣ 8, 84
Isa. 51:9-16   Heb. 11:8-16   John 7:14-31

Monday   56, 57,[58] ✣ 64, 65
Isa. 51:17-23   Gal. 4:1-11   Mark 7:24-37

Tuesday   61, 62 ✣ 68:1-20(21-23)24-36
Isa. 52:1-12   Gal. 4:12-20   Mark 8:1-10

Wednesday   72 ✣ 119:73-96
Isa. 54:1-10(11-17)   Gal. 4:21-31   Mark 8:11-26

Thursday   [70],71 ✣ 74
Isa. 55:1-13   Gal. 5:1-15   Mark 8:27—9:1

Friday   69:1-23(24-30)31-38 ✣ 73
Isa. 56:1-8   Gal. 5:16-24   Mark 9:2-13

Saturday   75, 76 ✣ 23, 27
Isa. 57:3-13   Gal. 5:25—6:10   Mark 9:14-29

Week of 5 Epiphany

Sunday   93, 96 ✣ 34
Isa. 57:14-21   Heb. 12:1-6   John 7:37-46

Monday   80 ✣ 77,[79]
Isa. 58:1-12   Gal. 6:11-18   Mark 9:30-41

Tuesday   78:1-39 ✣ 78:40-72
Isa. 59:1-15a   2 Tim. 1:1-14   Mark 9:42-50

Wednesday   119:97-120 ✣ 81, 82
Isa. 59:15b-21   2 Tim. 1:15—2:13   Mark 10:1-16

Thursday   [83] or 146, 147 ✣ 85, 86
Isa. 60:1-17   2 Tim. 2:14-26   Mark 10:17-31

Friday   88 ✣ 91, 92
Isa. 61:1-9   2 Tim. 3:1-17   Mark 10:32-45

Saturday   87, 90 ✣ 136
Isa. 61:10—62:5   2 Tim. 4:1-8   Mark 10:46-52

Week of 6 Epiphany

Sunday   66, 67 ✣ 19, 46
Isa. 62:6-12   1 John 2:3-11   John 8:12-19

Monday   89:1-18 ✣ 89:19-52
Isa. 63:1-6   1 Tim. 1:1-17   Mark 11:1-11

Tuesday   97, 99, [100] ✣ 94, [95]
Isa. 63:7-14   1 Tim. 1:18—2:8   Mark 11:12-26

Wednesday   101, 109:1-4(5-19)20-30 ✣ 119:121-144
Isa. 63:15—64:9   1 Tim. 3:1-16   Mark 11:27—12:12

Thursday   105:1-22 ✣ 105:23-45
Isa. 65:1-12   1 Tim. 4:1-16   Mark 12:13-27

Friday   102 ✣ 107:1-32
Isa. 65:17-25   1 Tim. 5:17-22(23-25)   Mark 12:28-34

Saturday   107:33-43, 108:1-6(7-13) ✣ 33
Isa. 66:1-6   1 Tim. 6:6-21   Mark 12:35-44

Week of 7 Epiphany

Sunday   118 ✣ 145
Isa. 66:7-14   1 John 3:4-10   John 10:7-16

Monday   106:1-18 ✣ 106:19-48
Ruth 1:1-14   2 Cor. 1:1-11   Matt. 5:1-12

Tuesday   [120], 121, 122, 123 ✣ 124, 125, 126, [127]
Ruth 1:15-22   2 Cor. 1:12-22   Matt. 5:13-20

Wednesday   119:145-176 ✣ 128, 129, 130
Ruth 2:1-13   2 Cor. 1:23—2:17   Matt. 5:21-26

Thursday   131, 132, [133] ✣ 134, 135
Ruth 2:14-23   2 Cor. 3:1-18   Matt. 5:27-37

Friday   140, 142 ✣ 141, 143:1-11(12)
Ruth 3:1-18   2 Cor. 4:1-12   Matt. 5:38-48

Saturday   137:1-6(7-9), 144 ✣ 104
Ruth 4:1-17   2 Cor. 4:13—5:10   Matt. 6:1-6

Week of 8 Epiphany

Sunday   146, 147 ✣ 111, 112, 113
Deut. 4:1-9   2 Tim. 4:1-8   John 12:1-8

Monday   1, 2, 3 ✣ 4, 7
Deut. 4:9-14   2 Cor. 10:1-18   Matt. 6:7-15

Tuesday   5, 6 ✣ 10, 11
Deut. 4:15-24   2 Cor. 11:1-21a   Matt. 6:16-23

Wednesday   119:1-24 ✣ 12, 13, 14
Deut. 4:25-31   2 Cor. 11:21b-33   Matt. 6:24-34

Thursday   18:1-20 ✣ 18:21-50
Deut. 4:32-40   2 Cor. 12:1-10   Matt. 7:1-12

Friday   16, 17 ✣ 22
Deut. 5:1-22   2 Cor. 12:11-21   Matt. 7:13-21

Saturday   20, 21:1-7(8-14) ✣ 110:1-5(6-7), 116, 117
Deut. 5:22-33   2 Cor. 13:1-14   Matt. 7:22-29

Week of Last Epiphany

Sunday   148, 149, 150 ✣ 114, 115
Deut. 6:1-9   Heb. 12:18-29   John 12:24-32

Monday   25 ✣ 9, 15
Deut. 6:10-15   Heb. 1:1-14   John 1:1-18

Tuesday   26, 28 ✣ 36, 39
Deut. 6:16-25   Heb. 2:1-10   John 1:19-28

Ash Wednesday   95 & 32, 143 ✣ 102, 130
Jonah 3:1—4:11   Heb. 12:1-14   Luke 18:9-14

Thursday   37:1-18 ✣ 37:19-42
Deut. 7:6-11   Titus 1:1-16   John 1:29-34

Friday   95 & 31 ✣ 35
Deut. 7:12-16   Titus 2:1-15   John 1:35-42

Saturday   30, 32 ✣ 42, 43
Deut. 7:17-26   Titus 3:1-15   John 1:43-51

Week of 1 Lent

Sunday 63:1-8(9-11), 98 ∴ 103
Deut. 8:1-10   1 Cor. 1:17-31   Mark 2:18-22

Monday 41, 52 ∴ 44
Deut. 8:11-20   Heb. 2:11-18   John 2:1-12

Tuesday 45 ∴ 47, 48
Deut. 9:4-12   Heb. 3:1-11   John 2:13-22

Wednesday 119:49-72 ∴ 49,[53]
Deut. 9:13-21   Heb. 3:12-29   John 2:23—3:15

Thursday 50 ∴ [59, 60] *or* 19, 46
Deut. 9:23—10:5   Heb. 4:1-10   John 3:16-21

Friday 95 & 40, 54 ∴ 51
Deut. 10:12-22   Heb. 4:11-16   John 3:22-36

Saturday 55 ∴ 138, 139:1-17(18-23)
Deut. 11:18-28   Heb. 5:1-10   John 4:1-26

Week of 2 Lent

Sunday 24, 29 ∴ 8, 84
Jer. 1:1-10   1 Cor. 3:11-23   Mark 3:31—4:9

Monday 56, 57, [58] ∴ 64, 65
Jer. 1:11-19   Rom. 1:1-15   John 4:27-42

Tuesday 61, 62 ∴ 68:1-20(21-23)24-36
Jer. 2:1-13   Rom. 1:16-25   John 4:43-54

Wednesday 72 ∴ 119:73-96
Jer. 3:6-18   Rom. 1:28—2:11   John 5:1-18

Thursday [70], 71 ∴ 74
Jer. 4:9-10, 19-28   Rom. 2:12-24   John 5:19-29

Friday 95 & 69:1-23(24-30)31-38 ∴ 73
Jer. 5:1-9   Rom. 2:25—3:18   John 5:30-47

Saturday 75, 76 ∴ 23, 27
Jer. 5:20-31   Rom. 3:19-31   John 7:1-13

Week of 3 Lent

Sunday 93, 96 ∴ 34
Jer. 6:9-15   1 Cor. 6:12-20   Mark 5:1-20

Monday 80 ∴ 77,[79]
Jer. 7:1-15   Rom. 4:1-12   John 7:14-36

Tuesday 78:1-39 ∴ 78:40-72
Jer. 7:21-34   Rom. 4:13-25   John 7:37-52

Wednesday 119:97-120 ∴ 81, 82
Jer. 8:18—9:6   Rom. 5:1-11   John 8:12-20

Thursday [83] *or* 42, 43 ∴ 85, 86
Jer. 10:11-24   Rom. 5:12-21   John 8:21-32

Friday 95 & 88 ∴ 91, 92
Jer. 11:1-8, 14-20   Rom. 6:1-11   John 8:33-47

Saturday 87, 90 ∴ 136
Jer. 13:1-11   Rom. 6:12-23   John 8:47-59

Week of 4 Lent

Sunday 66, 67 ∴ 19, 46
Jer. 14:1-9, 17-22   Gal. 4:21—5:1   Mark 8:11-21

Monday 89:1-18 ∴ 89:19-52
Jer. 16:10-21   Rom. 7:1-12   John 6:1-15

Tuesday 97, 99, [100] ∴ 94[95]
Jer. 17:19-27   Rom. 7:13-25   John 6:16-27

Wednesday 101, 109:1-4(5-19)20-30 ∴ 119:121-144
Jer. 18:1-11   Rom. 8:1-11   John 6:27-40

Thursday 69:1-23(24-30)31-38 ∴ 73
Jer. 22:13-23   Rom. 8:12-27   John 6:41-51

Friday 95 & 102 ∴ 107:1-32
Jer. 23:1-8   Rom. 8:28-39   John 6:52-59

Saturday 107:33-43, 108:1-6(7-13) ∴ 33
Jer. 23:9-15   Rom. 9:1-18   John 6:60-71

Week of 5 Lent

Sunday 118 ∴ 145
Jer. 23:16-32   1 Cor. 9:19-27   Mark 8:31—9:1

Monday 31 ∴ 35
Jer. 24:1-10   Rom. 9:19-33   John 9:1-17

Tuesday [120], 121, 122, 123 ∴ 124, 125, 126, [127]
Jer. 25:8-17   Rom. 10:1-13   John 9:18-41

Wednesday 119:145-176 ∴ 128, 129, 130
Jer. 25:30-38   Rom. 10:14-21   John 10:1-18

Thursday 131, 132, [133] ∴ 140, 142
Jer. 26:1-16   Rom. 11:1-12   John 10:19-42

Friday 95 & 22 ∴ 141, 143:1-11(12)
Jer. 29:1, 4-13   Rom. 11:13-24   John 11:1-27, *or* 12:1-10

Saturday 137:1-6(7-9), 144 ∴ 42, 43
Jer. 31:27-34   Rom. 11:25-36   John 11:28-44, *or* 12:37-50

Holy Week

Palm Sunday 24, 29 ∴ 103
Zech. 9:9-12**   1 Tim. 6:12-16**
Zech. 12:9-11, 13:1, 7-9***   Matt. 21:12-17***

Monday 51:1-18(19-20) ∴ 69:1-23
Jer. 12:1-16   Phil. 3:1-14   John 12:9-19

Tuesday 6, 12 ∴ 94
Jer. 15:10-21   Phil. 3:15-21   John 12:20-26

Wednesday 55 ∴ 74
Jer. 17:5-10, 14-17   Phil. 4:1-13   John 12:27-36

Maundy Thursday 102 ∴ 142, 143
Jer. 20:7-11   1 Cor. 10:14-17; 11:27-32
John 17:1-11(12-26)

Good Friday 95 & 22 ∴ 40:1-14(15-19), 54
Gen. 22:1-14   1 Peter 1:10-20   John 19:38-42***
John 13:36-38**

Holy Saturday 95 & 88 ∴ 27
Job 19:21-27a   Heb. 4:1-16**   Rom. 8:1-11***

Easter Week

Easter Day 148, 149, 150 ∴ 113, 114, *or* 118
Exod. 12:1-14**   ——   John 1:1-18**
Isa. 51:9-11***   Luke 24:13-35, *or* John 20:19-23***

Monday 93, 98 ∴ 66
Jonah 2:1-9   Acts 2:14, 22-32*   John 14:1-14

Tuesday 103 ∴ 111, 114
Isa. 30:18-21   Acts 2:36-41(42-47)*   John 14:15-31

Wednesday 97, 99 ∴ 115
Micah 7:7-15   Acts 3:1-10*   John 15:1-11

Thursday 146, 147 ∴ 148, 149
Ezek. 37:1-14   Acts 3:11-26*   John 15:12-27

Friday 136 ∴ 118
Dan. 12:1-4, 13   Acts 4:1-12*   John 16:1-15

Saturday 145 ∴ 104
Isa. 25:1-9   Acts 4:13-21(22-31)*   John 16:16-33

Week of 2 Easter

Sunday 146, 147 ∴ 111, 112, 113
Isa. 43:8-13   1 Pet. 2:2-10   John 14:1-7

Monday 1, 2, 3 ∴ 4, 7
Dan. 1:1-21   1 John 1:1-10   John 17:1-11

Tuesday 5, 6 ∴ 10, 11
Dan. 2:1-16   1 John 2:1-11   John 17:12-19

Wednesday 119:1-24 ∴ 12, 13, 14
Dan. 2:17-30   1 John 2:12-17   John 17:20-26

Thursday 18:1-20 ∴ 18:21-50
Dan. 2:31-49   1 John 2:18-29   Luke 3:1-14

Friday 16, 17 ∴ 134, 135
Dan. 3:1-18   1 John 3:1-10   Luke 3:15-22

Saturday 20, 21:1-7(8-14) ∴ 110:1-5(6-7), 116, 117
Dan 3:19-30   1 John 3:11-18   Luke 4:1-13

**Intended for use in the morning   ***Intended for use in the evening*

Week of 3 Easter

Sunday 148, 149, 150 ✲ 114, 115
Dan. 4:1-18 1 Pet. 4:7-11 John 21:15-25

Monday 25 ✲ 9, 15
Dan. 4:19-27 1 John 3:19—4:6 Luke 4:14-30

Tuesday 26, 28 ✲ 36, 39
Dan. 4:28-37 1 John 4:7-21 Luke 4:31-37

Wednesday 38 ✲ 119:25-48
Dan. 5:1-12 1 John 5:1-12 Luke 4:38-44

Thursday 37:1-18 37:19-42
Dan. 5:13-30 1 John 5:13-20(21) Luke 5:1-11

Friday 105:1-22 ✲ 105:23-45
Dan. 6:1-15 2 John 1-13 Luke 5:12-26

Saturday 30, 32 ✲ 42, 43
Dan. 6:16-28 3 John 1-15 Luke 5:27-39

Week of 4 Easter

Sunday 63:1-8(9-11), 98 ✲ 103
Exod. 28:1-4, 30-38 1 John 2:18-29 Mark 6:30-44

Monday 41, 52 ✲ 44
Exod. 32:1-20 Col. 3:18—4:6(7-18) Matt. 5:1-10

Tuesday 45 ✲ 47, 48
Exod. 32:21-34 1 Thess. 1:1-10 Matt. 5:11-16

Wednesday 119,49-72 ✲ 49, [53]
Exod. 33:1-23 1 Thess. 2:1-12 Matt. 5:17-20

Thursday 50 ✲ [59, 60] *or* 114, 115
Exod. 34:1-17 1 Thess. 2:13-20 Matt. 5:21-26

Friday 40, 54 ✲ 51
Exod. 34:18-35 1 Thess. 3:1-13 Matt. 5:27-37

Saturday 55 ✲ 138, 139:1-17(18-23)
Exod. 40:18-38 1 Thess. 4:1-12 Matt. 5:38-48

Week of 5 Easter

Sunday 24, 29 ✲ 8, 84
Lev. 8:1-13, 30-36 Heb. 12:1-14 Luke 4:16-30

Monday 56, 57, [58] ✲ 64, 65
Lev. 16:1-19 1 Thess. 4:13-18 Matt. 6:1-6, 16-18

Tuesday 61, 62 ✲ 68:1-20(21-23)24-36
Lev. 16:20-34 1 Thess. 5:1-11 Matt. 6:7-15

Wednesday 72 ✲ 119:73-96
Lev. 19:1-18 1 Thess. 5:12-28 Matt. 6:19-24

Thursday [70], 71 ✲ 74
Lev. 19:26-37 2 Thess. 1:1-12 Matt. 6:25-34

Friday 106:1-18 ✲ 106:19-48
Lev. 23:1-22 2 Thess. 2:1-17 Matt. 7:1-12

Saturday 75, 76 ✲ 23, 27
Lev. 23:23-44 2 Thess. 3;1-18 Matt. 7:13-21

Week of 6 Easter

Sunday 93, 96 ✲ 34
Lev. 25:1-17 James 1:2-8, 16-18 Luke 12:13-21

Monday 80 ✲ 77, [79]
Lev. 25:35-55 Col. 1:9-14 Matt. 13:1-16

Tuesday 78:1-39 ✲ 78:40-72
Lev. 26:1-20 1 Tim. 2:1-6 Matt. 13:18-23

Wednesday 119:97-120 ✲ ——
Lev. 26:27-42 Eph. 1:1-10 Matt. 22:41-46

Eve of Ascension —— ✲ 68:1-20
2 Kings 2:1-15 Rev. 5:1-14

Ascension Day 8, 47 ✲ 24, 96
Dan. 7:9-14 Heb. 2:5-18 Matt. 28:16-20

Friday 85, 86 ✲ 91, 92
1 Sam. 2:1-10 Eph. 2:1-10 Matt. 7:22-27

Saturday 87, 90 ✲ 136
Num. 11:16-17, 24-29 Eph. 2:11-22 Matt. 7:28—8:4

Week of 7 Easter

Sunday 66, 67 ✲ 19, 46
Ezek. 3:16-27 Eph. 2:1-10 Matt. 10:24-33, 40-42

Monday 89:1-18 ✲ 89:19-52
Ezek. 4:1-17 Heb. 6:1-12 Luke 9:51-62

Tuesday 97, 99, [100] ✲ 94, [95]
Ezek. 7:10-15, 23b-27 Heb. 6:13-20 Luke 10:1-17

Wednesday 101, 109:1-4(5-19)20-30 ✲ 119:121-144
Ezek. 11:14-25 Heb. 7:1-17 Luke 10:17-24

Thursday 105:1-22 ✲ 105:23-45
Ezek. 18:1-4, 19-32 Heb. 7:18-28 Luke 10:25-37

Friday 102 ✲ 107:1-32
Ezek. 34:17-31 Heb. 8:1-13 Luke 10:38-42

Saturday 107:33-43, 108:1-6(7-13) ✲ ——
Ezek. 43:1-12 Heb. 9:1-14 Luke 11:14-23

Eve of Pentecost —— ✲ 33
Exod. 19:3-8a, 16-20 1 Pet. 2:4-10

The Day of Pentecost 118 ✲ 145
Isa. 11:1-9 1 Cor. 2:1-13 John 14:21-29

Trinity Sunday 146, 147 ✲ 111, 112, 113
Job 38:1-11; 42:1-5 Eph. 4:1-16 John 1:1-18

The Season after Pentecost
Week of the Sunday closest to May 11

Monday 106:1-18 ✲ 106:19-48
Isa. 63:7-14 2 Tim. 1:1-14 Luke 11:24-36

Tuesday [120], 121, 122, 123 ✲ 124, 125, 126, [127]
Isa. 63:15—64:9 2 Tim. 1:15—2:13 Luke 11:37-52

Wednesday 119:145-176 ✲ 128, 129, 130
Isa. 65:1-12 2 Tim. 2:14-26 Luke 11:53—12:12

Thursday 131, 132, [133] ✲ 134, 135
Isa. 65:17-25 2 Tim. 3:1-17 Luke 12:13-31

Friday 140, 142 ✲ 141, 143:1-11(12)
Isa. 66:1-6 2 Tim. 4:1-8 Luke 12:32-48

Saturday 137:1-6(7-9), 144 ✲ 104
Isa. 66:7-14 2 Tim. 4:9-22 Luke 12:49-59

Week of the Sunday closest to May 18

Monday 1, 2, 3 ✲ 4, 7
Ruth 1:1-18 1 Tim. 1:1-17 Luke 13:1-9

Tuesday 5, 6 ✲ 10, 11
Ruth 1:19—2:13 1 Tim. 1:18—2:8 Luke 13:10-17

Wednesday 119:1-24 ✲ 12, 13, 14
Ruth 2:14-23 1 Tim. 3:1-16 Luke 13:18-30

Thursday 18:1-20 ✲ 18:21-50
Ruth 3:1-18 1 Tim. 4:1-16 Luke 13:31-35

Friday 16, 17 ✲ 22
Ruth 4:1-17 1 Tim. 5:17-22(23-25) Luke 14:1-11

Saturday 20, 21:1-7(8-14) ✲ 110:1-5(6-7), 116, 117
Deut. 1:1-8 1 Tim. 6:6-21 Luke 14:12-24

Week of the Sunday closest to May 25

Sunday 148, 149, 150 ✲ 114, 115
Deut. 4:1-9 Rev. 7:1-4, 9-17 Matt. 12:33-45

Monday 25 ✲ 9, 15
Deut. 4:9-14 2 Cor. 1:1-11 Luke 14:25-35

Tuesday 26,28 ✲ 36, 39
Deut. 4:15-24 2 Cor. 1:12-22 Luke 15:1-10

Wednesday 38 ✲ 119:25-48
Deut. 4:25-31 2 Cor. 1:23—2:17 Luke 15:1-2, 11-32

Thursday 37:1-18 ✲ 37:19-42
Deut. 4:32-40 2 Cor. 3:1-18 Luke 16:1-9

Friday 31 ✲ 35
Deut. 5:1-22 2 Cor. 4:1-12 Luke 16:10-17(18)

Saturday 30, 32 ✲ 42, 43
Deut. 5:22-33 2 Cor. 4:13—5:10 Luke 16:19-31

Week of the Sunday closest to June 1

Sunday	63:1-8(9-11), 98 ⁂ 103 Deut. 11:1-12 Rev. 10:1-11 Matt. 13:44-58
Monday	41, 52 ⁂ 44 Deut. 11:13-19 2 Cor. 5:11—6:2 Luke 17:1-10
Tuesday	45 ⁂ 47, 48 Deut. 12:1-12 2 Cor. 6:3-13(14—7:1) Luke 17:11-19
Wednesday	119:49-72 ⁂ 49,[53] Deut. 13:1-11 2 Cor. 7:2-16 Luke 17:20-37
Thursday	50 ⁂ [59, 60] *or* 8, 84 Deut. 16:18-20; 17:14-20 2 Cor. 8:1-16 Luke 18:1-8
Friday	40, 54 ⁂ 51 Deut. 26:1-11 2 Cor. 8:16-24 Luke 18:9-14
Saturday	55 ⁂ 138, 139:1-17(18-23) Deut. 29:2-15 2 Cor. 9:1-15 Luke 18:15-30

Week of the Sunday closest to June 8

Sunday	24, 29 ⁂ 8, 84 Eccles. 6:1-12 Acts 10:9-23 Luke 12:32-40
Monday	56, 57,[58] ⁂ 64, 65 Eccles. 7:1-14 Gal. 4:12-20 Matt. 15:21-28
Tuesday	61, 62 ⁂ 68:1-20(21-23)24-36 Eccles. 8:14—9:10 Gal. 4:21-31 Matt. 15:29-39
Wednesday	72 ⁂ 119:73-96 Eccles. 9:11-18 Gal. 5:1-15 Matt. 16:1-12
Thursday	[70], 71 ⁂ 74 Eccles. 11:1-8 Gal. 5:16-24 Matt. 16:13-20
Friday	69:1-23(24-30)31-38 ⁂ 73 Eccles. 11:9—12:14 Gal. 5:25—6:10 Matt. 16:21-28
Saturday	75, 76 ⁂ 23, 27 Num. 3:1-13 Gal. 6:11-18 Matt. 17:1-13

Week of the Sunday closest to June 15

Sunday	93, 96 ⁂ 34 Num. 6:22-27 Acts 13:1-12 Luke 12:41-48
Monday	80 ⁂ 77, [79] Num. 9:15-23; 10:29-36 Rom. 1:1-15 Matt. 17:14-21
Tuesday	78:1-39 ⁂ 78:40-72 Num. 11:1-23 Rom. 1:16-25 Matt. 17:22-27
Wednesday	119,97-120 ⁂ 81, 82 Num. 11:24-33(34-35) Rom. 1:28—2:11 Matt. 18:1-9
Thursday	[83] *or* 34 ⁂ 85, 86 Num. 12:1-16 Rom. 2:12-24 Matt. 18:10-20
Friday	88 ⁂ 91, 92 Numb. 13:1-3, 21-30 Rom. 2:25—3:8 Matt. 18:21-35
Saturday	87, 90 ⁂ 136 Num. 13:31—14:25 Rom. 3:9-20 Matt. 19:1-12

Week of the Sunday closest to June 22

Sunday	66, 67 ⁂ 19, 46 1 Samuel 4:12-22 James 1:1-18 Matt. 19:23-30
Monday	89:1-18 ⁂ 89:19-52 1 Samuel 5:1-12 Acts 5:12-26 Luke 21:29-36
Tuesday	97, 99 [100] ⁂ 94, [95] 1 Samuel 6:1-16 Acts 5:27-42 Luke 21:37—22:13
Wednesday	101, 109:1-4(5-19)20-30 ⁂ 119:121-144 1 Samuel 7:2-17 Acts 6:1-15 Luke 22:14-23
Thursday	105:1-22 ⁂ 105:23-45 1 Samuel 8:1-22 Acts 6:15—7:16 Luke 22:24-30
Friday	102 ⁂ 107:1-32 1 Samuel 9:1-14 Acts 7:17-29 Luke 22:31-38
Saturday	107:33-43, 108:1-6(7-13) ⁂ 33 1 Samuel 9:15—10:1 Acts 7:30-43 Luke 22:39-51

Week of the Sunday closest to June 29

Sunday	118 ⁂ 145 1 Samuel 10:1-16 Rom. 4:13-25 Matt. 21:23-32
Monday	106:1-18 ⁂ 106:19-48 1 Samuel 10:17-27 Acts 7:44—8:1a Luke 22:52-62
Tuesday	[120], 121, 122, 123 ⁂ 124, 125, 126, [127] 1 Samuel 11:1-15 Acts 8:1-13 Luke 22:63-71
Wednesday	119:145-176 ⁂ 128, 129, 130 1 Samuel 12:1-6, 16-25 Acts 8:14-25 Luke 23:1-12
Thursday	131, 132, [133] ⁂ 134, 135 1 Samuel 13:5-18 Acts 8:26-40 Luke 23:13-25
Friday	140, 142 ⁂ 141, 143:1-11(12) 1 Samuel 13:19—14:15 Acts 9:1-9 Luke 23:26-31
Saturday	137:1-6(7-9), 144 ⁂ 104 1 Samuel 14:16-30 Acts 9:10-19a Luke 23:32-43

Week of the Sunday closest to July 6

Sunday	146, 147 ⁂ 111, 112, 113 1 Samuel 14:36-45 Rom. 5:1-11 Matt. 22:1-14
Monday	1, 2, 3 ⁂ 4, 7 1 Samuel 15:1-3, 7-23 Acts 9:19b-31 Luke 23:44-56a
Tuesday	5, 6 ⁂ 10, 11 1 Samuel 15:24-35 Acts 9:32-43 Luke 23:56b—24:11
Wednesday	119:1-24 ⁂ 12, 13, 14 1 Samuel 16:1-13 Acts 10:1-16 Luke 24:13-35
Thursday	18:1-20 ⁂ 18:21-50 1 Samuel 16:14—17:11 Acts 10:17-33 Luke 24:36-53
Friday	16, 17 ⁂ 22 1 Samuel 17:17-30 Acts 10:34-48 Mark 1:1-13
Saturday	20, 21:1-7(8-14) ⁂ 110:1-5(6-7), 116, 117 1 Samuel 17:31-49 Acts 11:1-18 Mark 1:14-28

Week of the Sunday closest to July 13

Sunday	148, 149, 150 ⁂ 114, 115 1 Samuel 17:50—18:4 Rom. 10:4-17 Matt. 23:29-39
Monday	25 ⁂ 9, 15 1 Samuel 18:5-16, 27b-30 Acts 11:19-30 Mark 1:29-45
Tuesday	26, 28 ⁂ 36, 39 1 Samuel 19:1-18 Acts 12:1-17 Mark 2:1-12
Wednesday	38 ⁂ 119:25-48 1 Samuel 20:1-23 Acts 12:18-25 Mark 2:13-22
Thursday	37:1-18 ⁂ 37:19-42 1 Samuel 20:24-42 Acts 13:1-12 Mark 2:23—3:6
Friday	31 ⁂ 35 1 Samuel 21:1-15 Acts 13:13-25 Mark 3:7-19a
Saturday	30, 32 ⁂ 42, 43 1 Samuel 22:1-23 Acts 13:26-43 Mark 3:19b-35

Week of the Sunday closest to July 20

Sunday	63:1-8(9-11), 98 ⁂ 103 1 Samuel 23:7-18 Rom. 11:33—12:2 Matt. 25:14-30
Monday	41,52 ⁂ 44 1 Samuel 24:1-22 Acts 13:44-52 Mark 4:1-20
Tuesday	45 ⁂ 47, 48 1 Samuel 25:1-22 Acts 14:1-18 Mark 4:21-34
Wednesday	119:49-72 ⁂ 49, [53] 1 Samuel 25:23-44 Acts 14:19-28 Mark 4:35-41
Thursday	50 ⁂ [59, 60] *or* 66, 67 1 Samuel 28:3-20 Acts 15:1-11 Mark 5:1-20
Friday	40, 54 ⁂ 51 1 Samuel 31:1-13 Acts 15:12-21 Mark 5:21-43
Saturday	55 ⁂ 138, 139:1-17(18-23) 2 Samuel 1:1-16 Acts 15:22-35 Mark 6:1-13

Week of the Sunday closest to July 27		

Week of the Sunday closest to July 27

Sunday
24, 29 ⁛ 8, 84
2 Samuel 1:17-27　Rom. 12:9-21　Matt. 25:31-46

Monday
56, 57, [58] ⁛ 64, 65
2 Samuel 2:1-11　Acts 15:36—16:5　Mark 6:14-29

Tuesday
61, 62 ⁛ 68:1-20(21-23)24-36
2 Samuel 3:6-21　Acts 16:6-15　Mark 6:30-46

Wednesday
72 ⁛ 119:73-96
2 Samuel 3:22-39　Acts 16:16-24　Mark 6:47-56

Thursday
[70], 71 ⁛ 74
2 Samuel 4:1-12　Acts 16:25-40　Mark 7:1-23

Friday
69:1-23(24-30)31-38 ⁛ 73
2 Samuel 5:1-12　Acts 17:1-15　Mark 7:24-37

Saturday
75, 76 ⁛ 23, 27
2 Samuel 5:22—6:11　Acts 17:16-34　Mark 8:1-10

Week of the Sunday closest to August 3

Sunday
93, 96 ⁛ 34
2 Samuel 6:12-23　Rom. 14:7-12　John 1:43-51

Monday
80 ⁛ 77,[79]
2 Samuel 7:1-17　Acts 18:1-11　Mark 8:11-21

Tuesday
78:1-39 ⁛ 78:40-72
2 Samuel 7:18-29　Acts 18:12-28　Mark 8:22-33

Wednesday
119:97-120 ⁛ 81, 82
2 Samuel 9:1-13　Acts 19:1-10　Mark 8:34—9:1

Thursday
[83] or 145 ⁛ 85, 86
2 Samuel 11:1-27　Acts 19:11-20　Mark 9:2-13

Friday
88 ⁛ 91, 92
2 Samuel 12:1-14　Acts 19:21-41　Mark 9:14-29

Saturday
87, 90 ⁛ 136
2 Samuel 12:15-31　Acts 20:1-16　Mark 9:30-41

Week of the Sunday closest to August 10

Sunday
66, 67 ⁛ 19, 46
2 Samuel 13:1-22　Rom. 15:1-13　John 3:22-36

Monday
89:1-18 ⁛ 89:19-52
2 Samuel 13:23-39　Acts 20:17-38　Mark 9:42-50

Tuesday
97, 99, [100] ⁛ 94, [95]
2 Samuel 14:1-20　Acts 21:1-14　Mark 10:1-16

Wednesday
101, 109:1-4(5-19)20-30 ⁛ 119:121-144
2 Samuel 14:21-33　Acts 21:15-26　Mark 10:17-31

Thursday
105:1-22 ⁛ 105:23-45
2 Samuel 15:1-18　Acts 21:27-36　Mark 10:32-45

Friday
102 ⁛ 107:1-32
2 Samuel 15:19-37　Acts 21:37—22:16　Mark 10:46-52

Saturday
107:33-43, 108:1-6(7-13) ⁛ 33
2 Samuel 16:1-23　Acts 22:17-29　Mark 11:1-11

Week of the Sunday closest to August 17

Sunday
118 ⁛ 145
2 Samuel 17:1-23　Gal. 3:6-14　John 5:30-47

Monday
106:1-18 ⁛ 106:19-48
2 Samuel 17:24—18:8　Acts 22:30—23:11　Mark 11:12-26

Tuesday
[120], 121, 122, 123 ⁛ 124, 125, 126, [127]
2 Samuel 18:9-18　Acts 23:12-24　Mark 11:27—12:12

Wednesday
119:145-176 ⁛ 128, 129, 130
2 Samuel 18:19-33　Acts 23:23-35　Mark 12:13-27

Thursday
131, 132, [133] ⁛ 134, 135
2 Samuel 19:1-23　Acts 24:1-23　Mark 12:28-34

Friday
140, 142 ⁛ 141, 143:1-11(12)
2 Samuel 19:24-43　Acts 24:24—25:12　Mark 12:35-44

Saturday
137:1-6(7-9), 144 ⁛ 104
2 Samuel 23:1-7, 13-17　Acts 25:13-27　Mark 13:1-13

Week of the Sunday closest to August 24

Sunday
146, 147 ⁛ 111, 112, 113
2 Samuel 24:1-2, 10-25　Gal. 3:23—4:7　John 8:12-20

Monday
1, 2, 3 ⁛ 4, 7
1 Kings 1:5-31　Acts 26:1-23　Mark 13:14-27

Tuesday
5, 6 ⁛ 10, 11
1 Kings 1:38—2:4　Acts 26:24—27:8　Mark 13:28-37

Wednesday
119:1-24 ⁛ 12, 13, 14
1 Kings 3:1-15　Acts 27:9-26　Mark 14:1-11

Thursday
18:1-20 ⁛ 18:21-50
1 Kings 3:16-28　Acts 27:27-44　Mark 14:12-26

Friday
16, 17 ⁛ 22
1 Kings 5:1—6:1,7　Acts 28:1-16　Mark 14:27-42

Saturday
20, 21:1-7(8-14) ⁛ 110:1-5(6-7), 116, 117
1 Kings 7:51—8:21　Acts 28:17-31　Mark 14:43-52

Week of the Sunday closest to August 31

Sunday
148, 149, 150 ⁛ 114, 115
1 Kings 8:22-30(31-40)　1 Tim. 4:7b-16　John 8:47-59

Monday
25 ⁛ 9, 15
2 Chron. 6:32—7:7　James 2:1-13　Mark 14:53-65

Tuesday
26, 28 ⁛ 36, 39
1 Kings 8:65—9:9　James 2:14-26　Mark 14:66-72

Wednesday
38 ⁛ 119:25-48
1 Kings 9:24—10:13　James 3:1-12　Mark 15:1-11

Thursday
37:1-18 ⁛ 37:19-42
1 Kings 11:1-13　James 3:13—4:12　Mark 15:12-21

Friday
31 ⁛ 35
1 Kings 11:26-43　James 4:13—5:6　Mark 15:22-32

Saturday
30, 32 ⁛ 42, 43
1 Kings 12:1-20　James 5:7-12, 19-20　Mark 15:33-39

Week of the Sunday closest to September 7

Sunday
63:1-8(9-11), 98 ⁛ 103
1 Kings 12:21-33　Acts 4:18-31　John 10:31-42

Monday
41, 52 ⁛ 44
1 Kings 13:1-10　Phil. 1:1-11　Mark 15:40-47

Tuesday
45 ⁛ 47, 48
1 Kings 16:23-34　Phil. 1:12-30　Mark 16:1-8(9-20)

Wednesday
119:49-72 ⁛ 49, [53]
1 Kings 17:1-24　Phil. 2:1-11　Matt. 2:1-12

Thursday
50 ⁛ [59, 60] or 93, 96
1 Kings 18:1-19　Phil. 2:12-30　Matt. 2:13-23

Friday
40, 54 ⁛ 51
1 Kings 18:20-40　Phil. 3:1-16　Matt. 3:1-12

Saturday
55 ⁛ 138, 139:1-17(18-23)
1 Kings 18:41—19:8　Phil. 3:17—4:7　Matt. 3:13-17

Week of the Sunday closest to September 14

Sunday
24, 29 ⁛ 8, 84
1 Kings 19:8-21　Acts 5:34-42　John 11:45-57

Monday
56, 57, [58] ⁛ 64, 65
1 Kings 21:1-16　1 Cor. 1:1-19　Matt. 4:1-11

Tuesday
61, 62 ⁛ 68:1-20(21-23)24-36
1 Kings 21:17-29　1 Cor. 1:20-31　Matt. 4:12-17

Wednesday
72 ⁛ 119:73-96
1 Kings 22:1-28　1 Cor. 2:1-13　Matt. 4:18-25

Thursday
[70], 71 ⁛ 74
1 Kings 22:29-45　1 Cor. 2:14—3:15　Matt. 5:1-10

Friday
69:1-23(24-30)31-38 ⁛ 73
2 Kings 1:2-17　1 Cor. 3:16-23　Matt. 5:11-16

Saturday
75, 76 ⁛ 23, 27
2 Kings 2:1-18　1 Cor. 4:1-7　Matt. 5:17-20

Week of the Sunday closest to September 21

Sunday
93, 96 ** 34
2 Kings 4:8-37   Acts 9:10-31   Luke 3:7-18

Monday
80 ** 77, [79]
2 Kings 5:1-19   1 Cor. 4:8-21   Matt. 5:21-26

Tuesday
78:1-39 ** 78:40-72
2 Kings 5:19-27   1 Cor. 5:1-8   Matt. 5:27-37

Wednesday
119:97-120 ** 81, 82
2 Kings 6:1-23   1 Cor. 5:9—6:8   Matt. 5:38-48

Thursday
[83] or 116, 117 ** 85, 86
2 Kings 9:1-16   1 Cor. 6:12-20   Matt. 6:1-6, 16-18

Friday
88 ** 91, 92
2 Kings 9:17-37   1 Cor. 7:1-9   Matt. 6:7-15

Saturday
87, 90 ** 136
2 Kings 11:1-20a   1 Cor. 7:10-24   Matt. 6:19-24

Week of the Sunday closest to September 28

Sunday
66, 67 ** 19, 46
2 Kings 17:1-18   Acts 9:36-43   Luke 5:1-11

Monday
89:1-18 ** 89:19-52
2 Kings 17:24-41   1 Cor. 7:25-31   Matt. 6:25-34

Tuesday
97, 99, [100] ** 94, [95]
2 Chron. 29:1-3;   1 Cor. 7:32-40   Matt. 7:1-12

Wednesday
101, 109:1-4(5-19)20-30 ** 119:121-144
2 Kings 18:9-25   1 Cor. 8:1-13   Matt. 7:13-21

Thursday
105:1-22 ** 105:23-45
2 Kings 18:28-37   1 Cor. 9:1-15   Matt. 7:22-29

Friday
102 ** 107:1-32
2 Kings 19:1-20   1 Cor. 9:16-27   Matt. 8:1-17

Saturday
107:33-43, 108:1-6(7-13) ** 33
2 Kings 19:21-36   1 Cor. 10:1-13   Matt. 8:18-27

Week of the Sunday closest to October 5

Sunday
118 ** 145
2 Kings 20:1-21   Acts 12:1-17   Luke 7:11-17

Monday
106:1-18 ** 106:19-48
2 Kings 21:1-18   1 Cor. 10:14—11:1   Matt. 8:28-34

Tuesday
[120], 121, 122, 123 ** 124, 125, 126, [127]
2 Kings 22:1-13   1 Cor. 11:2, 17-22   Matt. 9:1-8

Wednesday
119:145-176 ** 128, 129, 130
2 Kings 22:14—23:3   1 Cor. 11:23-24   Matt. 9:9-17

Thursday
131, 132, [133] ** 134, 135
2 Kings 23:4-25   1 Cor. 12:1-11   Matt. 9:18-26

Friday
140, 142 ** 141, 143:1-11(12)
2 Kings 23:36—24:17   1 Cor. 12:12-26   Matt. 9:27-34

Saturday
137:1-6(7-9), 144 ** 104
Jer. 35:1-19   1 Cor. 12:27—13:3   Matt. 9:35—10:4

Week of the Sunday closest to October 12

Sunday
146, 147 ** 111, 112, 113
Jer. 36:1-10   Acts 14:8-18   Luke 7:36-50

Monday
1, 2, 3 ** 4, 7
Jer. 36:11-26   1 Cor. 13:(1-3) 4-13   Matt. 10:5-15

Tuesday
5, 6 ** 10, 11
Jer. 36:27—37:2   1 Cor. 14:1-12   Matt. 10:16-23

Wednesday
119:1-24 ** 12, 13, 14
Jer. 37:3-21   1 Cor. 14:13-25   Matt. 10:24-33

Thursday
18:1-20 ** 18:21-50
Jer. 38:1-13   1 Cor. 14:26-33a, 37-40   Matt. 10:34-42

Friday
16, 17 ** 22
Jer. 38:14-28   1 Cor. 15:1-11   Matt. 11:1-6

Saturday
20, 21:1-7 (8-14) ** 110:1-5 (6-7), 116, 117
2 Kings 25:8-12, 22-26   1 Cor. 15:12-29   Matt. 11:7-15

Week of the Sunday closest to October 19

Sunday
148, 149, 150 ** 114, 115
Jer. 29:1, 4-14   Acts 16:6-15   Luke 10:1-12, 17-20

Monday
25 ** 9, 15
Jer. 44:1-14   1 Cor. 15:30-41   Matt. 11:16-24

Tuesday
26, 28 ** 36, 39
Lam. 1:1-5(6-9)10-12   1 Cor. 15:41-50   Matt. 11:25-30

Wednesday
38 ** 119:25-48
Lam. 2:8-15   1 Cor. 15:51-58   Matt. 12:1-14

Thursday
37:1-18 ** 37:19-42
Ezra 1:1-11   1 Cor. 16:1-9   Matt. 12:15-21

Friday
31 ** 35
Ezra 3:1-13   1 Cor. 16:10-24   Matt. 12:22-32

Saturday
30, 32 ** 42, 43
Ezra 4:7, 11-24   Philemon 1-25   Matt. 12:33-42

Week of the Sunday closest to October 26

Sunday
63:1-8(9-11), 98 ** 103
Haggai 1:1—2:9   Acts 18:24—19:7   Luke 10:25-37

Monday
41, 52 ** 44
Zech. 1:7-17   Rev. 1:4-20   Matt. 12:43-50

Tuesday
45 ** 47, 48
Ezra 5:1-17   Rev. 4:1-11   Matt. 13:1-9

Wednesday
119:49-72 ** 49, [53]
Ezra 6:1-22   Rev. 5:1-10   Matt. 13:10-17

Thursday
50 ** [59, 60] or 103
Neh. 1:1-11   Rev. 5:11—6:11   Matt. 13:18-23

Friday
40, 54 ** 51
Neh. 2:1-20   Rev. 6:12—7:4   Matt. 13:24-30

Saturday
55 ** 138, 139:1-17(18-23)
Neh. 4:1-23   Rev. 7:(4-8)9-17   Matt. 13:31-35

Week of the Sunday closest to November 2

Sunday
24, 29 ** 8, 84
Neh. 5:1-19   Acts 20:7-12   Luke 12:22-31

Monday
56, 57, [58] ** 64, 65
Neh. 6:1-19   Rev. 10:1-11   Matt. 13:36-43

Tuesday
61, 62 ** 68:1-20(21-23)24-36
Neh. 12:27-31a, 42b-47   Rev. 11:1-19   Matt. 13:44-52

Wednesday
72 ** 119:73-96
Neh. 13:4-22   Rev. 12:1-12   Matt. 13:53-58

Thursday
[70], 71 ** 74
Ezra 7:(1-10) 11-26   Rev. 14:1-13   Matt. 14:1-12

Friday
69:1-23(24-30)31-38 ** 73
Ezra 7:27-28; 8:21-36   Rev. 15:1-8   Matt. 14:13-21

Saturday
75, 76 ** 23, 27
Ezra 9:1-15   Rev. 17:1-14   Matt. 14:22-36

Week of Sunday closest to November 9

Sunday
93, 96 ** 34
Ezra 10:1-17   1 Cor. 14:1-12   Matt. 20:1-16

Monday
80 ** 77, [79]
Joel 1:1-13   Rev. 18:15-24   Luke 14:12-24

Tuesday
78:1-39 ** 78:40-72
Joel 1:15—2:2(3-11)   Rev. 19:1-10   Luke 14:25-35

Wednesday
119:97-120 ** 81, 82
Joel 2:12-19   Rev. 19:11-21   Luke 15:1-10

Thursday
[83] or 23, 27 ** 85, 86
Joel 2:21-27   James 1:1-15   Luke 15:1-2, 11-32

Friday
88 ** 91, 92
Joel 2:28—3:8   James 1:16-27   Luke 16:1-9

Saturday
87, 90 ** 136
Joel 3:9-17   James 2:1-13   Luke 16:10-17(18)

Week of the Sunday closest to November 16

Sunday	66, 67 ∴ 19, 46	
	Hab. 1:1-4(5-11)12—2:1 Phil. 3:13—4:1 Matt. 23:13-24	
Monday	89:1-18 ∴ 89:19-52	
	Hab. 2:1-4, 9-20 James 2:14-26 Luke 16:19-31	
Tuesday	97, 99, [100] ∴ 94, [95]	
	Hab. 3:1-10(11-15)16-18 James 3:1-12 Luke 17:1-10	
Wednesday	101, 109:1-4(5-19)20-30 ∴ 119:121-144	
	Mal. 1:1, 6-14 James 3:13—4:12 Luke 17:11-19	
Thursday	105:1-22 ∴ 105:23-45	
	Mal. 2:1-16 James 4:13—5:6 Luke 17:20-37	
Friday	102 ∴ 107:1-32	
	Mal. 3:1-12 James 5:7-12 Luke 18:1-8	
Saturday	107:33-43, 108:1-6(7-13) ∴ 33	
	Mal. 3:13—4:6 James 5:13-20 Luke 18:9-14	

Week of the Sunday closest to November 23

Sunday	118 ∴ 145	
	Isa. 19:19-25 Rom. 15:5-13 Luke 19:11-27	
Monday	106:1-18 ∴ 106:19-48	
	Joel 3:1-2, 9-17 1 Pet. 1:1-12 Matt. 19:1-12	
Tuesday	[120], 121, 122, 123 ∴ 124, 125, 126, [127]	
	Nahum 1:1-13 1 Pet. 1:13-25 Matt. 19:13-22	
Wednesday	119:145-176 ∴ 128, 129, 130	
	Obadiah 15-21 1 Pet. 2:1-10 Matt. 19:23-30	
Thursday	131, 132, [133] ∴ 134, 135	
	Zeph. 3:1-13 1 Pet. 2:11-25 Matt. 20:1-16	
Friday	140, 142 ∴ 141, 143:1-11(12)	
	Isa. 24:14-23 1 Pet. 3:13—4:6 Matt. 20:17-28	
Saturday	137:1-6(7-9), 144 ∴ 104	
	Micah 7:11-20 1 Pet. 4:7-19 Matt. 20:29-34	